Dan & Pattie
1/17/23

The
CROSSING

Have the Best
day of your

life

L. Ashkarian (signature)

The CROSSING

Lela ASHKARIAN

Wasteland Press
Shelbyville, KY USA
www.wastelandpress.net

The Crossing
by Lela Ashkarian

First Printing—May 2009
ISBN: 978-1-60047-307-4

Printed in the U.S.A.

I dedicate this book to all the children of the world

PREFACE

The title of this book, *The Crossing*, represents many changes in my life. Some crossings have been geographical, as I traveled over vast oceans and continents far away from the land of my birth. Other crossings have been spiritual, as I grew from what I was taught as a child to how I believe today that God loves me and is my ever-present guide; these crossings came with the aid of spiritual advisors, priests, and my own reading and re-reading of the Bible.

There have been many crossings that relate to my business and career growth, taking me from an innocent secretary in Lebanon to a successful realtor in Florida, thanks in great part to my mentors and life coaches. Romantic crossings have been a little rocky, but from each one I learned a great deal about myself. I maintain eager expectation of one day finding a true and lasting love.

We manage the crossings in our life by faith. Each morning that we awake and start a new day is in itself a leap of faith. How much more faith does it take to cross an ocean or traverse a huge continent far away from all that is familiar to you? In Matthew 17:19-21, it says, "If ye have faith as a grain of mustard seed, and ye shall say unto this mountain, remove hence to yonder place; and it shall remove, and nothing shall be impossible unto you." That's a lot of faith!

When I looked back over my life and realized how many crossings had taken place and how much I learned along the way, I realized how important it was to share these life experiences and lessons with not only my family, friends, and business associates, but also anyone who would be interested in reading about them. This is my true story, much of it untold until now.

Take Time

Take time to think –
It is the source of all power.
Take time to read –
It is the fountain of wisdom.

Take time to play –
It is the source of perpetual youth.
Take time to be quiet –
It is the opportunity to seek God.

Take time to be aware –
It is the opportunity to help others.
Take time to love and be loved –
It is God's greatest gift.

Take time to laugh –
It is the music of the soul.
Take time to be friendly –
It is the road to happiness.

Take time to dream –
It is what the future is made of.
Take time to pray –
It is the greatest power on earth.

Take time to give –
It is too short a day to be selfish.
Take time to work –
It is the price of success.

Anonymous

1

A Turning Point

The deeper that sorrow carves into us,
The more joy we can contain.

Kahlil Gibran

WE MANAGE THE crossings in our life by faith. Each morning that we awake and start a new day is in itself a leap of faith. How much more faith does it take to cross an ocean or traverse a huge continent, far away from all that is familiar? It was January 1980, and I was about to receive the answer to that question.

Bernard had arrived in Beirut. I was busy finding a wedding dress and making plans for our small wedding, which was to take place in the St. Paul Orthodox Church in my home village of Anjar with just my immediate family in attendance. On the day of our wedding, it was snowing very hard. The roads were snow-covered and slick. I don't know how we made it from Beirut to Anjar, because in addition to the inclement weather, we had to pass through dangerous war zones and over high mountains. The ceremony was short and sad—sad especially for my parents because they knew it was a step toward my irrevocable departure from Lebanon.

After a week, I received a French visa, gathered up my few belongings, and we flew to France. On the plane, a strange feeling came over me. Where was I going with this man that I loved so madly but knew so little about? We were married. I had taken a serious step. I should have paid closer attention to that still, small voice inside of me.

We arrived in Paris that night, and the next day we took a TGV high-speed train to his village between St. Etienne and Montbrison. I was so tired from not having slept well the night before that I could have fallen asleep on a bed of rocks. Bernard put me up in a little hotel not far from his house. He told me he would get his car and return. I wondered why he wasn't taking me to meet his family right away, but being so tired, I fell fast asleep as soon as he left. I dreamed about a woman toasting me, and my glass broke in my hand.

At that precise moment, there was a knock at the door. When I opened it, there stood Bernard, panting heavily. He was very nervous as he blurted out, "Get ready. We must go to Lyon immediately." I packed my things, and we left. In my confusion, I simply followed his instructions. After we checked into a hotel in Lyon, I sat on the bed, and he knelt on the floor before me. He told me how much he loved me, but…but…

"But what?" I asked innocently.

"I'm married, and I have two daughters."

I felt his words like a physical blow. I was devastated. Tears ran down my cheeks. I was hyperventilating. I didn't know what to do. I only knew that my entire world had just crashed down around me.

This romance that turned sour so suddenly was a turning point in my life. Turning points are opportunities to initiate the powerful process of self-renewal. "See yourself as a champion, a victor," my mother used to tell me. I was still to learn that the crisis of losing a man I loved so intensely was in fact pointing me toward a new destination that was not on any road or any map.

2

Do You See the Stars?

Beyond a wholesome discipline,
Be gentle with yourself.
You are a child of the universe,
No less than the trees and stars;
You have a right to be here,
And whether or not it is clear to you,
No doubt the universe is unfolding as it should.

Max Ehrmann, "Desiderata"

THE DARKNESS OF night arrived, but the sky was ablaze with millions of stars clearly visible in the tiny village of Anjar. No artificial lights detracted from this heavenly panorama. The air was cool and crisp. My father and I lay on a handmade mattress on our stone front porch surrounded by berry, almond, and fig trees, with the family vineyard nearby. Punctuating the clear night air was the pungent odor of cow dung; we lived next to a barn. The crickets chirped their nightly songs, and a large ant stung my soft skin as it went about his chore of gathering tiny remnants of my father's fall harvest.

"You see those stars?" my father asked, nudging me to attention. As we watched the stars that seemed to get brighter and closer, he told me that we become stars when we die. "When I pass from this life, I will watch over you and protect you from above. Just look up at the stars and know that I am one of them looking out for you."

I was born on May 31, 1957. I was not given a name at birth. In fact, I lived for forty days without a name. My mother told me that I struggled to stay alive after a neighboring Arab woman cast an evil spell on me. The custom in such a case is to gather little wood chips from the ground where the evildoer has walked, passing over the same ground seven times, and then burning them together with incense and amid prayers.

I was on the verge of dying. My parents were out gathering the wood chips when a woman named Leila Karageozian came to our house. She was the daughter of a wealthy philanthropist from New York. She saw me about to take my last breath and asked my parents if she could hold me and give me her name. They called the priest, who baptized me as Leila Dilabazian, and after that I quickly recovered.

I saw my godmother only twice after that. Once, when I was in kindergarten, she gave me a piece of dark chocolate. The next time I saw her, I was studying for my governmental examination in 1972. I spoke only broken English at that time, but I tried to tell her about the legend of El Dorado. I was very ambitious. I wanted to be covered in gold. I wanted to reach the top of the mountain and touch the stars. Leila gently responded, "Next time I see you, I hope you will be married and have children." I cringed at that, because I didn't want to get married at an early age, as was expected in my culture. I wanted to get an education.

Anjar is a village of about five-thousand people located in the Bekaa Valley, an area of fertile farmland that sprawls between Beirut and the Syrian capital, Damascus. In fact, the main road connecting those two capitals passes right through Anjar. The only village in Bekka constructed according to a mapped-out plan, Anjar has the shape of a soaring eagle, its wings fully extended in flight. The air is clean, and the climate is dry with hot summers and cold winters.

The rich red soil of the Bekka has enabled farmers to turn the region into a green paradise. Anjar is known for its apples; there are hundreds of apple orchards! Our two-room house was built of concrete. One of the rooms had a tin roof. When it rained, the rain dripped on us, but for us children it was great fun sleeping under that tin roof and hearing the rain splatter it rhythmically. The only source of heat in our house was an oil-burning stove. A kerosene lamp was my light, and when the kerosene burned out, it was time for me to go to bed. My older sisters had to study by candlelight.

As a child, I always carried a stick in my hand and rode it like a horse. I would chase anything that crawled in that dry summer heat. One day when I was walking around, I picked up something thinking it was a yellow stick, but it was a yellow snake! Still, I was not afraid. Nor was I afraid of darkness. Whenever my mother saw me approaching, she would say, "Here comes the philosopher," because I always commented on what other people said. My father called me "the Arabian horse" because I stamped my feet on the ground when I walked.

I was born an Orthodox Christian, although my family didn't attend church together. My mother went to church by herself, while my father prayed at home every morning, turning his face to the East and raising his hands to the heavens. When I was fourteen, I invited Jesus to take hold of my hand and join me in my life's journey. I imagined growing up walking with Him. This was the foundation of my lifelong commitment to Christ. My friends and I attended St. Paul Orthodox Church until the ninth grade, but in 1974, I converted to the Evangelical faith and attended that church. My family didn't object.

I attended the Armenian Gulbenkian College in Anjar from kindergarten to the ninth grade. I loved school and my friends in Anjar. We didn't have the kind of amusements that kids have today, but we found great pleasure playing during the summer months. Almost every day after school and during study breaks, we would play hopscotch, hide-and-seek, and treasure hunt. We also made our own kites and squealed with delight as we watched them flutter high in the air. After my conversion to the Evangelical Church, I attended the Armenian Evangelical High School, where I graduated with honors.

Growing up, I was quite the tomboy. I rode horses into the Lebanese mountains near Anjar and enjoyed participating in sports, playing ping-pong and basketball with my village team in the Armenian athletic league. I belonged to the Girl Scouts until I was twenty-two years of age. During the summer months, I often went on camping trips and jamborees in neighboring villages. I was also one of the first women in the village to drive a car. No one objected to my driving, but my uncle objected to my biking and horseback riding, since, according to popular culture, these activities endangered the hymen. He even objected to my playing basketball because of the short shorts we wore.

As a young girl, I used to hum and sing a song about a wandering soul:

Little vagabond on the empty road,
Traveling in a land far away.
You sing a melody of tunes that call from home.
Go, vagabond, wherever you can.
When you sleep, take the rock for your head,
The cactus for your pillow.

My mother used to tell me to stop singing that song, because she knew that one day I would leave her.

My dreams of life beyond Anjar became more real when I was thirteen years old. I met a boy named Hagop (Jack), whose family came from Baghdad. He attended my school temporarily while his family awaited their American visas. Jack was my puppy love. He was gorgeous and tall, with skin as white as snow, curly hair, and large almond-shaped hazel eyes, and he was skilled at basketball. He knew English and introduced me to reading. English books were scarce; I even went door to door in search of them.

I became an avid reader of magazines such as *National Geographic* and *Reader's Digest*, as well as biographies and translations of the works of Russian authors—anything that gave me hope that one day I could flee Anjar. I was infatuated with America. I used to read aloud, thinking that I was speaking English. I even read to the walls when no one was watching.

Soon it was time for Jack's family to leave Anjar for America. I dedicated the next seven years of my life to seeing him again. We communicated, first often and then seldom, as so often happens in long-distance friendships. I used to watch for the mailman, hoping that he had a letter for me from Jack. I finally received only one or two letters a year, and then the mail stopped coming altogether.

3

A Rich Ancestral History

It is important to honor our beginnings,
To remember that we matter,
And that we have a place in this world
That no one else has.

Anonymous

MY ANCESTRY IS important to me. By learning about it, I have learned a great deal about myself. I feel that my strength derives from the stamina of the early Armenians, even though their lives were far different from my own, filled with hardships that I can barely imagine. These resilient people, whose bloodlines connect with mine, inspire me to persevere against all odds, as they did.

My passion for life, friends, family, good health, fitness, and work comes from the passion that always has been characteristic of Armenian women. We embrace life with great gusto and are unrestrained in the expression of our feelings. We are also long on patience and endurance.

At the height of its long and troubled history, the ancient Armenian kingdom covered five-hundred-thousand square miles of fertile plains from the Black Sea to the Caucasus Mountains to Persia and Syria. The land is beautiful, but rugged. Mount Ararat, the highest peak, rises eight thousand feet above sea level. Many rivers, including the Euphrates and the Tigris, flow through this region, watering green fields, orchards, and vineyards, eventually spilling into the Caspian Sea, the Black Sea, and the Persian Gulf. Called the cradle of mankind, this land has instilled in Armenians a strong sense of personal dignity and national pride, feelings that still run deep no matter where they reside.

Armenians have been oppressed and persecuted throughout history. From 1915 to 1923, the Turks perpetrated genocide against them, centrally planned and administered by the government. The Armenian people were subjected to deportation, expropriation, abduction, torture, massacre, and starvation. The great bulk of the population was forcibly removed from Armenia and deported to Syria, where the vast majority died of hunger and thirst in the desert. It is estimated that more than one and a half million Armenians perished in those years. Thousands of churches, schools, and community institutions were destroyed or confiscated. The entire wealth of the Armenian people was expropriated. The destruction of the Armenian communities in Asia Minor and historic West Armenia was total. My grandparents were among those thousands who were massacred by Turkish invaders.

In 1915, the Austrian Jewish author and poet, Franz Werfel, wrote *The Forty Days of Musa Dagh*, a famous novel about the heroic battle of the people of Musa Dagh. It tells how the young Turkish government of the Ottoman Empire, of which Musa Dagh (also called Jebel Musa, or Mountain of Moses), was a part, how they tried to eliminate ethnic Armenians, and how the Musa Daghians resisted deportation to the Syrian desert, taking shelter on the Mountain of Moses, and fighting off the regular armies of the Ottoman Empire for forty days. Their defeat was only a matter of time, however. They put a white flag with a red cross on it on top of the mountain so that ships in the Mediterranean might notice them, and indeed, the warships of the French Navy noticed the sign. They bombarded the Ottoman units and saved the people from extermination. The Musa Daghians brought the flag with them when they left their homeland.

During the French Mandate, the Musa Daghians stayed in Bassit, Syria, while arrangements were made to secure a home for them. While there, many of the Armenian refugees suffered and died from infectious diseases. In 1928, the French Mandate in Syria and Lebanon appointed a committee to reorganize the dry desert land in Lebanon. The French authorities donated land in

Anjar to all the displaced Musa Daghians and the Armenian immigrants of the Alexandrette region.

My paternal grandmother feeding the chickens

Movses der Kalousdian, the famous hero of the Forty Days of Musa Dagh and later a member of the Syrian Parliament (1927-1937), played a vital role in securing a location and transferring the displaced immigrants from the Bassit seaside to the semi-desert, dusty plains on the eastern mountain range of Lebanon, near the eastern border of Lebanon and Syria. Finally, the French Navy helped them to relocate, first by ships from Bassit to Tripoli, a northern Lebanese port, and then by cargo trains to the central rail station of Rayak in the Bekaa. Finally, they were trucked to the barren plains of Anjar and were issued maps that confirmed their ownership of the land. The exodus was completed on September 14, 1939.

These historical events profoundly affected the future generations of people in Anjar. Every year, in mid-September, the Anjarians, as well as Musa Daghians the world over, celebrate the anniversary of the heroic battle of Musa Dagh. The holiday is known as the Day of the Cross because of the cross on the flag that saved the people. Many male infants born in the week of this celebration bear the name Khatchig or Khachadour, which literally means "cross" or "given by the cross."

The Bekaa then was vastly different from the fertile farmlands found there today. Anjar, officially known as Haouch Moussa, was a disappointing contrast to Musa Dagh. Gone were the lush greens of the mountains and the sweet smell of orange groves. Instead, these brave refugees found a dry, dusty land, occupied by insects and disease. The hasty exodus of the Musa Daghians from their mountain homeland and their arrival to the barren plains of Anjar created tragic cases in virtually every family. People were homesick, hungry, cold, and demoralized.

One of the first major problems of the Armenian refugees was food. They had no means to cultivate the land. Some mules and oxen were rented from the neighboring villages. The first crops of Anjar were barley and corn. People had to make flour from these grains into bread dough and bake it. This bread was torturous to chew. It hardened like stone after it was baked.

Before any houses were built, the Armenian General Benevolent Union distributed tents, and with them the refugees erected a tent village on the hilly ashes of the Khalkis ruins. Aside from adjusting to the rigors of living in a barren desert with inadequate housing and food, the first Anjarians faced the serious catastrophe of malaria. In the primitive tent village, makeshift toilets were made of wood. Infectious dysentery also ravaged the population. More than eight hundred of the original settlers lost their lives in this epidemic, including one of my uncles. Priests spent entire days at the local cemetery, and no church bell ringing was permitted for the dead.

Malaria caused panic in the weakened population. Something had to be done in order to overcome the epidemic by whatever means. A French Army medical doctor was brought in to help people deal with disease, and a local medical volunteer team helped distribute medical supplies. Everyone was forced to take quinine, and hygiene "police" taught residents to keep their homes clean.

On September 20, 1939, the construction of houses began. The original plan was to build family houses with two rooms and a toilet for each family. When World War II started, this plan was downsized for financial reasons to allow for only one 4 x 4.5 meter room and an adjacent toilet. Some of these rooms still exist in Anjar. They are known as the "French Rooms." Over a thousand such rooms were constructed at a cost of three-thousand French francs each. The housing land for each family was four-hundred square meters. This gave the future generations the base on which to build housing plots.

In addition to building the first houses, the French established a field hospital in Deir Zanoun. The Antilias Holy Seat pleaded with Armenian organizations everywhere for help. The Armenian Red Cross built a maternity ward.

Anjar was plagued with mosquitoes. The Karageozian Foundation helped dig trenches and canals to drain the swamps and provide DDT. My godmother Leila Karageozian was the founder of this foundation, which was instrumental in establishing a new clinic for children up to age thirteen. In 1963, the Armenian Relief Society opened a clinic, as well.

Winters were especially harsh, and most of the women and children were sent to the neighboring Arab villages of Majdel-Anjar, Bar-Ilias, Saouiry, Raouda, Kab-Ilias, Mrayjat, Terbol, and Kfarzabad for shelter and food. Anjarians will be forever grateful to their Arab neighbors for their traditional hospitality.

In the first year, Anjar had no potable running water, so people were obliged to carry all the water they needed on their shoulders from the spring of Dzardager, a kilometer north of the village. Later, fountains were built to ease burden of the women carrying water on muddy roads in summertime and snow-covered roads in winter.

I lived with no running water until the day I left Anjar for Beirut in quest of education and improved living conditions. Although we had no indoor plumbing, we did have electricity and TV. Watching the popular program, "Dallas," I imagined living a better, richer, and more abundant life somewhere over the ocean in a place called America.

By 1943, Anjarians had started a small farm and began to develop other small industries to serve the growing municipality. First, a small shoe factory opened, and then some people began making combs, while others worked on "dazgahs," or traditional carpet weaving. The first years were tough but the Musa Daghians proved to be tougher.

My maternal grandmother separating the chaff from the grain

Today, what once was a barren land stands transformed into a fertile valley, full of trees and farms, orchards, vineyards, and large beautiful homes. Approximately two-thousand-four-hundred people, the vast majority of them Armenian, live in Anjar, which has its own municipality, including a mayor, regional representatives, and a city council. Now, Anjar has become a tourist destination. In the spring, people picnic and dine on local trout. In the summer people visit the Umayyad ruins.

My heart is full of love and appreciation for the early Anjarians. Like other Armenians, I am forever indebted to these early refugee settlers, which included my parents. Their example has given me the strength to persevere in the face of hardships and serves as a reminder to me that only through adversity one can acquire the courage and strength to persevere in the face of life's challenges.

4

Family Ties

So much of what is best in us
Is bound up in our love of family,
That it remains the measure of
Our stability because it measures
Our sense of loyalty. All other pacts
Of love or fear derive from it and
Are modeled upon it.

Haniel Long

MY PARENTS WERE born in the shadow of Jebel Musa, the Mountain of Moses, in Turkey. When they were young, they became refugees, fleeing the genocide of their friends, families, and compatriots, more than a million in all. They endured harsh weather, inadequate food, poor sanitary conditions, and disease, arriving in Anjar, weak, sick, and destitute. Although my parents didn't speak Turkish, every now and then I remember that they would quote a Turkish proverb: "*Kismetinden Baska Bir sey Olmaz*," which means, "Nothing happens unless it is predestined." That proverb framed their life, from hardship to happiness.

My parents were always struggling. They had a couple of cows, an apple orchard, pear trees, and a vineyard that produced magnificent, plump, juicy grapes. They also used some land for growing wheat and barley.

My mother and aunts

My mother used to tell us stories about when she was very young. She was the eldest child in her family; they lived through harsh frozen winters and hot summers in the Anjarian tent city.

My mother loved music and singing. Her favorite popular singers were Engelbert Humperdinck and Tom Jones. A woman with no education, she once told me how her mother drew letters in the sand to teach her the Armenian alphabet. She was also known far and wide for her beautiful needlework. She became a master at crocheting. Although she was illiterate, she could pick up a magazine, look at a garment, count the stitches, and reproduce it perfectly. People were amazed at her handiwork and came from as far as the United States and Canada to purchase it.

A short, stocky woman with big hazel eyes and long white hair, her size belied her strength. In our home, she was a general in command, strict and quick to hand out discipline. Her words were strong, loud, and clear. Whatever she said, that settled it! She was just as quick to break out in laughter, no matter what the situation was. She gained many friends and lost family relationships because she was authentic and truthful to the bone.

She did many jobs: milking the cows, cutting grass to feed them, and harvesting wheat, apples, plums, grapes, and peaches. She also was the seamstress of the village. She sewed school uniforms and dancers' costumes. In our culture, girls were not supposed to ride bicycles, much less horses, or to climb mountains. But mother encouraged me to do all these things and more. She promised me that as long as she could, she would support my schooling and social activities. I shared with her my dreams of being free, studying what I wanted, going to college and driving a nice car, living lavishly, having beautiful things, traveling to the ends of the earth, and doing good deeds. I promised to take her with me all around the world, but it never happened because she didn't want to leave my brother.

Mother was a good cook. I ate whatever I was served, because we had few choices in those days. Once, however, when I was visiting a well-to-do friend, she didn't like what her mother had prepared for her dinner, so she ignored the meal and instead made a pot of French fries. I fell in love with French fries until one day when I came home and saw that my mother had prepared our daily staple, bulgar pilaf. I sneaked into the kitchen and started to peel a couple of potatoes.

"What do you think you are doing?" my mother asked.

"I don't like what you have prepared for us," I said with the same arrogant attitude as my friend. "Instead, I will fry these potatoes." That was it. The whole plate, potatoes and peelings, landed in front of our cows in a flash. My mother regretted having done that to me until the day she died. She would cry every time she saw me when I visited her on my occasional trips to Lebanon. "I could cut my hands for what I did to you that day," she would say to me. But I was grateful that she acted as she did, because it taught me to appreciate what I have.

One other time that my mother disciplined me was during a trip to the neighboring town of Zahle. Our father used to take us there when he sold apples. During these occasions, he would buy us only what was absolutely necessary, like shoes or maybe a pair of trousers. On this particular trip, my parents took me with them. I was probably nine or ten at the time. I saw a red-fringed hat, and wanted it so badly that I started to have a fit, the way children sometimes do to get their way. In response, my mother slapped me so hard with the back of her hand that blood came rushing from my mouth. "From now on," she snapped, "if you say 'I want,' you will never get anything!" Those words immediately sunk into my subconscious; never again did I ask anything of my parents.

During the years I spent in Korea and Japan, my mother kept my letters and pictures in her Bible under her pillow. Every time I visited Lebanon for vacation, she would greet me with a big smile, her eyes brimming with tears. She would be happy the first couple of days; then, as the days passed, she would seclude herself and cry secretly, praying that she would see me again, because she knew that there would be a good-bye.

My mother seldom got angry with me, no matter what I said, which surprised my siblings with whom she often argued. When she caught me crying over my first, failed love affair, she said, "I can understand and feel your pain, because I've been there." I was shocked and surprised at this statement. For a moment, I forgot my pain and asked her about her life. She told me that she had fallen in love with a man, but didn't marry him because when she and my father were teenagers, their parents had arranged for them to be engaged. After that, they were not allowed to see one another for fourteen years.

My father standing tall on the barren land in Lebanon

My father, Hovannes Dilabazian, was the only son in his family. His father had been slaughtered during the Armenian genocide in Turkey. His mother was a Ghassanid. The Ghassanids were a South Arabian Christian tribe, a group of which emigrated in the early third century from Yemen to the Hauran in southern Syria. They also settled in Jordan and the Holy Land, where they intermarried with Hellenized Roman settlers and other Greek-speaking people in the early Christian communities.

My father stood a bit taller than most Armenian men. Besides tending the farm, he worked for other people, separating wheat grain from chaff. He would leave the house around 4 a.m. and return late at night. He also sold cattle, fruits, vegetables, olives, olive oil, and real estate. He was a wheeler and dealer. Despite our meager existence, occasionally we would sit down to a huge feast. The large table would be weighted down by all sorts of homegrown foods. My father would carve the lamb, and all of us would enjoy the rich bounty and each other's company.

In my youth, I was unaware that my father gave food to less fortunate families. He would take a bushel of apples and give it to a neighboring Arab. He didn't speak about having done such things, but he left his mark on others, regardless of whether they knew about his generosity or not.

My father had a darker side, however. He beat my mother with his fists when he got angry—typical behavior for Lebanese men in those days—although he never laid hands on his children.

My parents' relationship was a puzzle to me. My father would tremble with anxiety when my mother got sick. He would show love to her in many ways, but she would not accept it. When he tried to caress her, she would elbow him away. When I was growing up I wondered how he could love her, yet beat her. Once, when I was in the eleventh grade, he was about to hit her. "I'll poison you if you touch her again!" I shouted. When he raised his fist to hit me, I challenged him, saying, "Go ahead. Do it." He looked me in the eyes and dropped his hand. He never hit my mother after that.

My father was a dream weaver. He would talk about a faraway country named America. Although he had never been to America, he told me how it rained there. To my father, rain was important; it nourished his land and meant the only prosperity he ever knew.

"When there is rain, there is food," he used to tell me. Father was a great storyteller, although he had a foul mouth. I used to laugh at his swearing. He had many Arab friends from nearby villages who would come almost every night and sit around the table, munching our nuts and dried figs, listening to his stories.

Although my father was illiterate, he succeeded in sending five children to school. I was the only one, however, that graduated from college. My father pulled my elder sisters, Mary and Madeline, out of school and put them into arranged marriages. My eldest sister Mary entered into an arranged marriage to an Armenian. I was five or six years old at the time. Mary is a very pretty, quiet, obedient, godly woman, who has been blessed with four intelligent and successful children.

Mary has had a life full of hardships and suffering, raising her children under emotionally and financially stressful circumstances, but she succeeded in educating them in a way that has brought her happiness and satisfaction. Her children are not only well educated and respectful, but also fully aware of the sacrifices their mother made to help them achieve their life goals.

God has always shown His powerful presence in Mary's life. Seven years ago she was diagnosed with cancer, and today her surgeon cannot control his emotions every time he sees her. "That's impossible! It's a miracle!" he shouts. "We didn't expect you to live more than six months after your operation." Her elder daughter, who was then pregnant, prayed day and night for her mother to live long enough to see her first grandchild. She not only lived to see her, but she took full care of her until she went to kindergarten. Mary's strong faith to God and endless love of life and the people around her gave her a second life. Now she lives with her elder son and his family, takes care of household chores, cooks, cleans, and baby-sits with great enthusiasm and joy.

Madeline, my second oldest sister, is a very hardworking, strict woman who is very much a perfectionist. She doesn't like to see mistakes! One plus one equals two. That's it! No discussion, no arguments. She wants everything to be in order. She is very neat and tidy, and a great cook. She is also an accomplished dancer and singer, and has many artistic abilities.

Little Lela with my brothers and sisters

When she was in school, she was judged the best folk dancer and was offered a scholarship to follow her dream of folk dancing, but my father gave her a choice: either she stopped dancing or she went to school. My sister was so hardheaded that she declared she wouldn't do either. Thus, she put an end to an important dream that might have led to her advancement in life; for many years, she lived a very secluded life until she married. She has three children, now all married with children of their own.

When I left Anjar to continue my studies in Beirut, I stayed with Madeline for four years during which she was like a mother to me, doing all her best to make me feel at home.

Annie, my third sister, was born with abnormal feet. My mother had to carry her on her back until she was twelve years old. When she was nineteen, she underwent several operations with the help of the Red Cross, but she still suffers from this handicap. Despite her physical problems, she has grown to be a strong, persistent, and humorous nurse, who is ready to help and give comfort to anyone who needs it. She also takes care of her single daughter and sick husband.

Arranged marriages worked for my two eldest sisters, and might have worked for me, too. I believe that pre-negotiated marriages tend to be more stable than modern marriages, which suffer from such high divorce rates. While all three of my sisters are still married, I was the only one whom the stability of married life has eluded. I am a childless woman, and suffered for over twenty years because of this. Finally, after many years of guilt, self-condemnation, and self-pity, I asked God to take this pain from my heart. I am grateful that my prayers have been answered.

My final sibling is my brother Khatchig. My mother used to call him "Pasha" and gave him favored treatment in the family. He was always given the best part of any meal. My mother used to sit by the front door waiting for him to come home early in the morning when he had been out at night. If she didn't see him for a day, she would practically stop breathing. Her son was her entire life. Khatchig was caring, giving, and gentle as a lamb. He provided for all my sisters and brothers during the war, and opened his doors to all who could fit into his house, giving them shelter, food, and money.

5

The Other Side of the Mountain

The greatest thing in this world
Is not so much where we are,
But in what direction we are moving.

Oliver Wendell Holmes

M Y PARENTS DID whatever they could to afford me the opportunities for the highest education possible. After I received my first baccalaureate in Anjar, I wanted to go to Beirut for further education. At that time, Beirut was riveted by civil war between Muslims and Christians. From Anjar, we could see the Beirut port burning fifty miles away. I remained in Anjar for a year while fierce fighting raged in Lebanon. I helped my parents with their farming, tending the house, and fruit picking. I also coached the basketball team at my high school.

The top university in the Middle East is the American University of Beirut, where the faculty is American and classes are taught in English. I wanted to attend it to study to be a nurse. To qualify, I needed to have two baccalaureates, the equivalent of a degree from a junior college. As the 1975 school season approached, I decided to stay with my sister Madeline while I worked toward my second baccalaureate in Arabic philosophy.

My mother had wanted to sell her one and only milking cow to enable me to attend AUB. I objected and told her I would rather work to put myself through school. I promised her that when I graduated, I would put my graduation robe on her; and that is precisely what I did nineteen years later.

After receiving my second baccalaureate, I taught for a year in a prestigious private Armenian school. I taught English, modern mathematics, and civics. I was a young, vibrant, tenacious, and popular teacher, and approached my job with a passion. To help make ends meet, I also worked as a tutor.

In 1979, however, I decided to change careers, and joined a company that took care of the automated car-wash machines for the entire Lebanese market. There, I worked for Antoine Hage, a Lebanese-American gentleman, who taught me to run his office efficiently while he was in Saudi Arabia. Mr. Hage was a man of great integrity, honesty, and patriotism. He not only promised to make me the best secretary on Earth, but he also sent me to school to learn international accounting and secretarial skills.

To collect the mail, I had to go from East Beirut to the central post office, located in the western part of the city. At that time, the so-called Green Line, dividing Christians from Muslims, separated Beirut into two sectors. Snipers tried to prevent anyone from crossing. To avoid dangerous zones, I zigzagged around buildings and skirted the port, avoiding bomb craters and masked vigilantes. The majority of car-wash customers were wealthy Muslims living in West Beirut. To meet them, I had to pass through Sabra and Shatila, the Palestinian refugee camps where a massacre occurred in 1982. Many times I dodged sniper fire and deftly eluded artillery shelling. I would park my car on the side of the road and seek safety until I thought it would be safe to pass the Green Line.

One day, when I was the only person on the road, two masked men dressed as civilians came out of nowhere from both sides of the road. They ordered me to stop, and with one man on each side of my car, they began interrogating me. "Where are you coming from? What do you do for a living? Who do you work for?" Eventually, they let me go on my way.

On another occasion, while I was working at the office, bombs started exploding all around. I rushed out, jumped into my car and started crisscrossing through what was supposed to be a safe Armenian neighborhood. As I entered the street, a rocket came right behind me. Through my rear mirror, I could see human body pieces flying through in the air. I left the car in the middle of the street and found shelter. After staying there a couple of hours, I made my way to my sister's house. She and her family were happy to see me in one piece but were horrified that the war was on their doorstep.

Neighbors said that the Christian Phalangists were shanghaiing Armenian men between nineteen and forty-five and making them join their militia. The first floor of my sister's building was the safest place to stay. My sister was pregnant with her third child. I told her and her husband, "I have no children. Go down to the first floor, and I'll bring you food." For two weeks, I climbed to their apartment on the fifth floor, first using a flashlight, later using candles, to retrieve food. But we began to run out of bread and canned goods. To feed the children I cooked a mixture of flour, sugar, and water.

A cease-fire was declared. I was able to look into the mirror for the first time in two weeks; my hair had turned white. I believe that this period of horror, depression, and malnutrition caused me to develop a thyroid problem, first diagnosed in 1985. The cease-fire fell to pieces a month later. I went back to my sister and her family on the first floor of her building and resumed my treks to the fifth floor. The situation repeated itself time and again. I wasn't afraid, however, because I knew that the God within me was greater than any worldly adversaries.

In 1979, I was sitting in Madeline's living room when I heard the doorbell. It was my friend Mary, who was several years older than me, beautiful, very knowledgeable, and fluent in five languages. She asked if I wanted to go out to dinner with her, her boyfriend, and one of his friends. At that time, I was not in a relationship, so I said yes. Mary's boyfriend's guest that evening was a man from France by the name of Bernard. As we proceeded to a local restaurant, I rode in front with Mary's boyfriend, and Bernard sat in back with Mary. Since I didn't know a word of French, Mary was more than willing to serve as our interpreter that evening. As we conversed, I looked into the rearview mirror, and the first time I saw Bernard's big, black, deep-set eyes, my heart started pounding. He was very good looking, with his dark hair and his dark eyes.

All the signs and sounds of war were around us—barricades, pockmarked buildings, burned-out cars, and smoldering fire—but that night we were oblivious. With the war serving as a backdrop to our young romance, we wanted to dine and dance the night away, living life to the hilt. I did have a midnight curfew, which Madeline set, but I missed it that night. Instead, I slept on a chair in Bernard's rented flat in the western, mostly Muslim-occupied side of Beirut.

Bernard and I exchanged promises early on. He would teach me French, and I would teach him English. That was the beginning of a very intense romance that involved much more than language lessons! Every day, we went out together. I used to go to the main post office in the heart of the dangerous war zone to pick up Bernard's mail. I prayed that if he were a good man, God would see us through these terrible times.

I became completely enmeshed in Bernard's love and lovemaking. His passion ignited the woman in me, and I willingly surrendered my virginity to him at the age of twenty-two. He taught me not just how to make love but how to make the most of the subtle nuances of lovemaking to fully satisfy him and me. I was madly in love. The mere sound of Bernard's name would send waves of warmth washing over my entire body. Being apart was sheer agony. I would go for days without eating. I was not hungry for food; I was hungry for Bernard.

In a year, I learned to speak French like a Parisian, because, after all, I was in love with a Frenchman and wanted to communicate with him verbally as much as with my other senses. Our love was soon to be tested, however, for he was sent to Hanoi to work in his field of telecommunications engineering. Where would I go? How would I break the news to my family that I was no longer a virgin and that I wanted to follow my lover to the ends of the earth?

In my culture, when a woman loses her virginity outside of marriage, it dooms her to unmarried life forever. What had I done? Despite the ominous overtones of my actions, I suffered no immediate recriminations. Instead, I began looking seriously for a job outside of Lebanon for the sole purpose of running away from my problem rather than being mature and confronting it. I found myself at the crossroads of crises—the painful experiences of war, my lover being far away, my parents living in Anjar, and I, living with my sister, brother-in-law and their three children in a very small house. That juncture was a defining moment for me.

One day while reading the newspaper, I saw an advertisement for a job in Saudi Arabia. By then, I had become so disgusted with the ongoing Lebanese civil war that I wanted to flee Lebanon and make something of myself somewhere else, all the while maintaining my dream to one day live in America. I applied for the job and received an answer to my application from Santa Monica, California. I packed my things during a fierce bombardment in Beirut, crossed the Green Line, and stayed with a friend of mine who had gone to high school and played basketball with me. The road to the Beirut airport was closed; no planes were arriving or departing.

Faced with no other choice, the company that hired me decided that we would travel by land. They made several cars available to transport us, and we crossed the Shouf Mountains, and then continued through the mountains of Lebanon and into Syria. En route, I could see my village from the main road to Syria but I couldn't stop to say good-bye to my parents who hadn't seen me for a while. I cried to myself and swallowed my tears.

I was the only Christian woman traveling with thirteen Muslim nurses who were relocating to Saudi Arabia. It was midnight when we reached the border of Jordan and Damascus. The border soldiers thoroughly investigated us and in doing so, they found among my possessions a Bible, couple of dictionaries, and an album full of pictures of Bernard, my family, and my friends. They asked me if I was a spy; of course I replied that I was not. I explained that I was going to work in Saudi Arabia by invitation of the International Medical Enterprises (IME) that was under contract with the Saudi Military Hospital.

After checking our belongings and interrogating us, they finally let us go. We stayed in Jordan for a couple of nights, and then we flew to Jeddah. My fellow travelers were transported from Jeddah to Taif by car, but they flew me to Taif. Because I was a Christian, they didn't want me to travel in a vehicle passing through the holy cities of Mecca and Medina.

I worked for the Medical Consultancy for almost a year. While there, I stayed in a prince's villa rented by my employer. I served primarily as the company's telex operator, but I also prepared medical manuals. I met some very nice people, including American doctors and management people who trained me in the American way of thinking and working.

Some of my prayers were being answered, but meanwhile I was waiting for news from Bernard. I knew that he was in Hanoi, but I had no idea that one day, out of the blue, he would contact me from Ivory Coast in Africa. I was working that day, and my manager brought me a letter from him. I took a deep breath, as if I had been breathless for a long time and was now breathing again. I opened his letter, kissed it, read it, re-read it, slept with it, and kept it tightly next to me at all times.

Bernard's absence had left me with contradictory feelings. In one way, I was empty without him. He had filled my life with all the manifestations of love—gentle caresses, soft and sensuous kisses, passionate lovemaking, and the constant assurance of his physical presence. On the other hand, I was so much in love that even in Bernard's absence, in the quiet of my room at night, just thinking of him and reminiscing how he made love to me was sufficient to bring orgasmic waves over me. *How powerful love is*, I thought.

Bernard wanted me to meet him in Ivory Coast. I immediately started preparing my passport to go on holiday there. I did everything that the Ivory Coast Embassy requested of me, but still they wouldn't grant me a visa to visit him there. Finally, I decided to leave Saudi Arabia altogether. I had grown weary of working long hours and feeling sad with my family so far away. I decided to return to Lebanon. Meanwhile I spoke with Bernard about visiting me in Beirut.

With plans underway to quit my high-paying job in Saudi Arabia and return to Lebanon, I also devised other plans. Bernard and I would get married and leave Lebanon forever. Of course, my parents were against this idea, but I was so much in love. I told them that if I didn't marry Bernard, I would kill myself. How impetuous are the young when they are in love!

So it was that I found myself in that hotel room in Lyon. After finally telling me the truth, Bernard explained that he would have to leave me at the hotel, but would return in a couple of days. I was petrified, breathless. I felt weak, and sadness consumed me. I didn't eat for days. At one point in my sorrow, I felt that I was having a heart attack. I had fallen so blindly in love with Bernard that I had forgotten who I was. I cried day and night. Finally, he returned with a plan. He wanted me to rent a place in Lyon until we could find a way to leave France and go to Madagascar, where he would find work as a telecommunications engineer.

Bernard was a persuasive man. Everything seemed possible with him. He said he wanted to take me with him, even though he was married and had children. He said he didn't love his wife. He asked me to be his mistress and live with him in Madagascar. It was difficult for me to refuse his offer, as I was still very much in love with him, but I was no longer blindly in love. With my eyes wide open, I said no to him. Bernard already had sent my passport to the Madagascar Embassy, so I made arrangements to retrieve it.

After staying in France for a month, I met some Armenians near my apartment, and they were very comforting and helpful. I finally called my brother to ask for forgiveness. He asked me if I was pregnant, and when I told him I wasn't, he said I could come home and the family would accept me.

In January 1982, I returned to Anjar. I was taking Valium to sleep and forget my pain. I ached all over physically, emotionally, and spiritually. My mother sat with me and encouraged me, repeating her own sad love story, and how life worked out for her in the long run.

My maternal grandmother was then in her eighties. She used to visit me every day. When she saw me sleeping all the time, she asked my mother why, and my mother told her what had happened. Finally, my grandmother nudged me to do an about-face and emerge from my sadness. Her advice to me was, "Stand up straight. Be rooted, grounded. Put your red dress on, and your red lipstick; act as if nothing has happened, so that our neighbors will see you strong and stop gossiping. Otherwise, they will capitalize on your weakness."

This lesson of turning a negative into a positive is one that has been reinforced many times in my life since then. When I did as she suggested, I learned that how I saw and felt about myself would have a tremendous impact on how far I would go in this life toward fulfilling my destiny. Self-image is so important. When we think we are successful, knowledgeable, faithful, and committed to God's plan, the result of our efforts will be positive. Knowing that I am a unique individual, I feel grateful for the person I am, rather than trying to be someone else. I know I have weaknesses and make mistakes, but I keep working to improve myself so that my self-image will become ever more like God's image of me.

It's important for us to learn to love ourselves on the basis of who we are, not what we do. When we believe in ourselves and have faith that we can do better and bigger things because of who we are, we can succeed. It helps to have another person, a mentor like my mother and grandmother were for me, to open our eyes to see our strengths to endure whatever circumstances we face. We have to see ourselves as champions, as victors. "At least you learned the French language and have seen France," my mother told me after I returned home in tears. We need to express our love to others. The inner cause is more precious than the outward effect. Robert Southwell said it so perfectly, "Not where I breathe, but where I love, I live."

6

Civil War – And a New Love

All forms of violence, especially war,
Are totally unacceptable as means
To settle disputes between and among
Nations, groups, and persons.

Dalai Lama

I WAS READY to start life again in Lebanon. Back in Beirut, I rented a room in a convent. At that time, June 1982, the Lebanese war was fierce. Bashir Gemayel was president, and the Syrians were in Beirut. In addition, the Israeli invasion was at hand. I was quickly hired to represent a reputable company at an office machinery exhibition. The owner of the company was a wealthy Iraqi who had a printing house and imported English language books to universities and ministries. He was the Middle East representative, and he selected me to attend an international book fair at Mosul University in Iraq.

I went with my best girlfriend, a Palestinian. Working the book fair was difficult, as books were censored, and I had to be careful what I said and which books I presented. At this time, Saddam Hussein's forces were fighting Iran with the support of the United States. We could hear the bombing. "My goodness," I said to my girlfriend, "we ran away from Lebanon and now here we are again." We have a saying, "I ran away from the rain but got caught in the hail."

After couple of weeks, we returned to Beirut. I decided that I needed to work for an organization that would pay me an adequate salary for my services, so I prepared my résumé and sent it to American Embassy, UNICEF, and Caterpillar. I was particularly interested in working at the U.S. Embassy, however. After my interview and six weeks of a security clearance check, I got the job. I was hired to be a translator, secretary, and filing clerk.

Only those who have watched their country being torn apart and devastated by war can understand the pain I suffered watching the beautiful city of Beirut shelled and bombed, its infrastructure and architectural masterpieces rendered to dust and destruction. Beirut had once enjoyed a golden age, when travelers from around the globe sought out its glitz and glamour. Known as the Paris of the Middle East, it had been a magnet for the wealthy. Overlooking the deep blue Mediterranean, its magnificent beaches set amid a backdrop of snowcapped mountains, it enjoyed peace and prosperity as an international tourist attraction and banking center. People of all faiths lived and worked side by side.

The Lebanese Civil War, which began in 1975, completely divided the city, which was now overwhelmed by factions — Sunnis, Shiites, Maronites, Palestinians, Druze, and other groups— all vying for control. Many residents fled to safer parts of the country when most services collapsed. Power and water were in short supply, and garbage was dumped into a landfill in the sea, just opposite the hotel district.

On June 6, 1982 Israel invaded Lebanon in an attempt to rout the leaders of the Palestinian Liberation Organization (PLO), operating out of Beirut. When the PLO leaders refused to surrender and barricaded themselves in West Beirut, Israel bombarded the city. In the wake of the destruction, many innocent people were killed or wounded, including hundreds of Palestinians slaughtered by Christian Phalangists in the Sabra and Shatila refugee camps. Israeli Ariel Sharon, considered the architect of the invasion, forced the PLO to evacuate to Tunisia, while the Israelis eventually withdrew to southern Lebanon.

In the next two years, from 1982 to 1984, the Multinational Force (MNF), comprised of French, Italian, American, and British troops, was stationed in Beirut. They became the target of many attacks, including two bombings on October 23, 1983 that killed up to three hundred members of the U. S. and French forces. By early 1984, the MNF had left Beirut. In 1986, the Lebanese government, representing a coalition of many factions, invited the Syrian government to send troops to suppress the fighting in Beirut. That invitation opened the doors to governmental instability and continued destruction. The fighting in Beirut continued through 1990.

During 17 years of civil war, Lebanon lost its economy and its culture. The war left scars on the minds and bodies of children who had never experienced life without bombs and shells. Children there did not reach for toys or dolls; they reached for guns. Soldiers looted stores and homes. People crowded two, four, six families into two rooms. Families huddled in bomb shelters and passed days and nights without sunshine. As a result of my own experience of the war, I developed a deep yearning for the simplicity and peace of village life that was lost during this tragic time.

Early in the 1990s, greater stability finally took hold, and some very ambitious plans were undertaken to start rebuilding this truly magnificent city. Indeed, like the fabled phoenix, Beirut rose from the ashes of war and transformed itself. The infrastructure was rebuilt, first-class hotels were opened, nightclubs welcomed returning Lebanese and visitors alike, and life slowly returned to some semblance of normalcy.

Life in Lebanon would never be quite the same, however. During the war, many Lebanese fled not only to other, safer parts of Lebanon but also to other parts of the world. They established businesses, married, had children, and settled down. After the war, many of them chose not to return to their beloved homeland except as occasional tourists.

On April 18, 1983 at approximately 1:00 p.m., a suicide bomber driving a delivery truck packed with about two thousand pounds of explosives detonated a car bomb in front of the American Embassy in Beirut. The van, believed to have been stolen from the embassy a year earlier, gained access to the compound and parked under the portico at the very front of the building, where it exploded.

The blast collapsed the entire central façade of the horseshoe-shaped building, leaving the wreckage of balconies and offices in heaped tiers of rubble and spewing masonry, metal, and glass fragments far and wide. The explosion was heard throughout West Beirut and broke windows as far as a mile away. Rescue workers worked around the clock for days, unearthing the dead and wounded.

A total of sixty-three people were killed in the blast: thirty-two Lebanese employees, seventeen Americans, and fourteen visitors and passersby; one hundred and twenty or more people were also wounded. Eight of the Americans worked for the CIA, and included the CIA's top Middle East analyst and Near East director, Robert Ames, and the entire Middle East contingent of the CIA.

The American Embassy staff, which included me, was evacuated to relative safety. Following the bombing, we were unable to return to the embassy to work, but the British Embassy allowed us to set up our offices there, and so I was able to keep my job.

Richard Allen, an American telecommunications engineer with USAID, was helping to splice the shreds of Lebanon's communications system back together. We met quite by chance at in the summer of 1983 while I was partying in a hotel. He asked me if I would show him the city. As we were crossing from one sector of Beirut to another, a militiaman seized Richard's American passport for no apparent reason. "Without a passport, you're dead," I told Richard. I then turned to the guard and said, "This man is helping our country. If you want to keep his passport you can shoot me in the heart." I was looking directly at a gun aimed at my chest. I felt no fear. After some hesitation, the guard returned Richard's passport.

Richard and I continued dating, having coffee, lunch, and dinner together, and going on some other social outings. We liked each other a lot and began dating seriously. I would spend nights at his beachfront apartment. He was an excellent cook and a fantastic underwater diver who belonged to the Jacques Cousteau Society. His life dream was to sail around the world alone under the stars.

February 4, 1984 was Richard's birthday, which we celebrated that night. The next day, we left for work, crossing the Green Line into western Beirut, where the embassy was located. We then parted, each going our separate ways to our respective jobs. I always kept all my necessary belongings, some clothing, money, and jewelry, my passport, and my school papers in my Samsonite briefcase. It was important to take such precautions in case something happened and we could not retrieve them on an emergency exit from the country.

For lunchtime, I wanted to have a tuna sandwich with my colleagues. We passed through the barricades to a little hole-in-the-wall restaurant where we purchased our lunch. On our way back to our office, we were showered with bombs and rockets. Not knowing the direction of the attacks, we crawled on the ground like snakes, praying that we could escape the shelling.

Some young U. S. Marines behind the sandbag barricades called to us and let us stay ducked down with them for several hours until sundown. Then we went to the American Embassy for shelter. The bombing persisted; we could hear it falling right and left and all around the embassy. Terrified, hungry, confused, and not knowing how long this might continue, we took shelter in a corner of a room in the office building. All the while, I was wondering and worrying about how Richard was doing and where he was hiding.

I dialed Dorothy Simmons, a friend who worked in the political section of the embassy to see if I could stay with her after the bombing was over before crossing the Green Line again to go back home. I talked with her for a few minutes and was relieved to hear that she was in a safe place. Then phone lines then went down, and we were completely cut off from the rest of the world. Later we found out that Dorothy's house had been bombed. The rocket went through the apartment, passing through a room in which I had once stayed, and damaging everything. Dorothy's cat was the only living creature in the apartment that survived.

Richard was in the nearby Rivera Hotel, a few minutes away from the embassy, but he could not leave to come and see me. The bombing stopped on the fourth day of our siege after the militias let the Muslim employees leave the embassy. The authorities at the embassy decided to let all their local employees go, and the Americans were ordered to leave Lebanon.

The following morning, I was standing at the entrance of the embassy waiting to hear how I could get out when suddenly I saw

Richard and the other engineers with whom he worked lining up to get on board a helicopter. I got a chance to say good-bye to Richard. He gave me a necklace that he used to wear, with a piece of eight (an old Spanish coin) at the end of it. "Take this necklace as an engagement ring," he said, "and I promise that I'll come back for you."

I was heartbroken, however, at the thought that I would never see him again, and wondered if I had lost the second love of my life to circumstances beyond my control. Then I watched as Richard climbed into a helicopter taking him to the USS Guam, a battleship anchored off the coast. From there, he was evacuated to Nicosia, Cyprus. I cried night and day, and when there were no more tears, I would ask God, "Why is this happening to me?"

7

Escape from Lebanon

When we long for life without difficulties,
Remind us that the mighty oak grows
Strong in contrary winds, and diamonds
Are made from extreme pressure.

Rev. Peter Marshall

O N FEBRUARY 8, 1984, I was cowering in the basement of the embassy under fierce shelling in the city, along with a handful of Armenian Christian employees, the Muslim employees already having been evacuated. At 11:05 p.m., I wrote a letter to Richard through my tears, at times barely able to see the paper. I told him that after he left our apartment had been bombed, and that there was heavy shelling all over Jounieh, Beirut's eastern port.

"Baby, I don't think I can make it," I wrote. "I think I'm going to die. Just remember that somebody in your life loved you and that you loved me in return. My tears won't allow me to continue. If my writing is full of mistakes, it's because my eyes are full of tears. Not even the best Beaujolais can put a smile on my face."

Finally, we were transported to the Christian side of Beirut by helicopter. Fortunately, I had my passport with me, along with some jewelry and necessary paperwork that I always carried with me in case of an evacuation. I left my car in front of the American Embassy and jumped into the chopper. When I got out, I checked my earrings. The right one was missing. Before Richard had left, I had had a dream about losing an emerald earring, which had been on my right ear!

The helicopter took us to Jounieh. My friends had called their parents to pick them up, but I had nowhere to go, no family with a car to come and pick me up. I decided to take a taxi to Richard's beach apartment, talk with this landlord, and get some of his belongings. From there, I found my way to a telephone and began contacting hotels in Nicosia. The first one I tried was the Hilton. I asked if Richard was staying at the hotel, and the answer came back, yes! I then telexed Richard. "Take the next boat to Cyprus," he replied. "I am waiting."

I headed for the wharf at the edge of the port. Flinging myself up the gangway of a dirty cargo ship, I managed to get on board headed for Cyprus, still wearing the same clothes I had worn a week earlier. I hadn't taken a shower or combed my hair. I didn't dare look at my face in the mirror; I knew I must have looked scary. Surely I would have frightened myself.

On board the rusty old vessel, I slept only minutes in the fourteen hours of the storm-tossed trip. Many people, desperate and broken-hearted like me, lined the deck, but most of the time we huddled in the ship's hold. It had been six days since the bombing started, and I had eaten only M&Ms, crackers, and a few cans of food. Yet, throughout this ordeal, I remained mindful of Ephesians 3:20, "The will of God will never take you where the grace of God will not protect you." I knew in my heart of hearts that I was in alignment with God's plan and would have His protection.

It was a cold day in February when we arrived in Larnaca. I knew that I had to have some money to get to Nicosia, but I didn't want to give the taxi driver the two-hundred dollars that I was carrying for Richard. So I hired a driver who drove me to the Hilton, where the American Embassy personnel and USAID contractors were staying en route to US. It took half an hour to get there, and as I was getting out of the car I told the driver that I didn't have any money for the fare, but that I would give him my gold and diamond ring. He refused to take it, and we parted with mutual blessings.

When I arrived in the hotel lobby, people were shocked and surprised to see me. I was reunited with Richard and finally managed to take a shower in the hotel and get a good night's sleep. I didn't know where I would go from there. A day or two later, Richard told me that he had a plan. He would go to United States to finish some personal business. He asked me to stay behind in Cyprus for a few days.

We went to the British Embassy, and I called a British friend of mine, Debbie Van Kholer, and asked her if I could stay with her for a few weeks until I could join Richard in the States. She agreed, and my joy was immeasurable.

Debbie and I had worked together in Saudi Arabia. She was childless, and I had attempted to arrange for her to adopt a child from Lebanon, but had not succeeded. We went to the British Embassy and applied for a visa. This was not easy to get in those days, but with the help of an embassy employee, I managed to obtain one.

Bristol, England was cold and gloomy when I first arrived there on February 14, 1984. All I had with me were a pair of jeans and a lightweight jacket. Debbie clothed me, fed me, and took me to Cornwall, where we stayed with her mother for a month. I missed my family terribly. In the evenings, my pillow was drenched with tears for my loved ones: my sisters, my brother, nieces and nephews, and my mom and dad. They didn't know where I was, even though I tried to call them. Telephones were scarce and expensive in Lebanon. No lines were open, so I tried to send cards. On dark nights, all I could think about was going to the United States. I constantly prayed and knew that angels were guiding and protecting me.

En route to America, my imagination went wild. As a child, I used to dream of driving on the streets of Los Angeles. I had read a book by Emile Coue, a French pharmacist who astonished the world around 1920 with the results he obtained with the power of autosuggestion. I won my first brand new car by this method. At the time, I was a young teacher struggling to make ends meet in Lebanon. I would longingly eye my friends' and neighbors' vehicles and wonder if I would ever save enough money to acquire a new car.

One day, I returned from tutoring exhausted, yet focused on my dream that one day I would be behind the wheels of a new car. That night, I dreamed about three double-digit numbers. I purchased three tickets from an elementary school fundraising event and, lo and behold, I won the brand new Toyota Corolla! I had been so sure that I was going to win that I told other people to burn their tickets!

In the same way, my determination and perseverance enabled me to cross the Mediterranean as war raged in my homeland. I never wanted to return, and I prayed that I would never have to go back. I left my family, friends, and culture, but I knew that I had to sacrifice those things for the chance to live in a better, more peaceful, and harmonious environment. I understood that the dynamic of change is inevitable and unstoppable. I wanted a change of environment so much that I was willing to leave everything that I had known behind. Life is a series of good-byes, but on the other side are hellos. My intuition and spirit were leading me. I knew I was going to be in a better situation and have a better life. I was twenty-seven years old, and the wind was blowing my sail, taking me into a new direction.

What I learned from this experience was, as Rabindrinath Tagore once said, "The winds of Grace are always blowing. It is you who must raise your sails." Our habit of thinking can be a prison or a paradise. We need to guard our thinking always, for whatever we think about affects our feelings, which in turn affects our actions. Whatever we think about we talk about, and whatever we talk about we bring about. By guarding our thoughts and planting the right seeds in our mind, we will get the results we want in life.

Whoever we may be, regardless of how big a failure we may think ourselves to be, the power to do what we need to do to be happy and resourceful is within us. Because our actions follow our feelings and thoughts, this power to do things we never dreamed possible becomes available to us as soon as we change our beliefs.

8

America, At Last!

If you have built castles in the air,
Your work need not be lost;
That is where they should be.
Now put the foundations under them.

Henry David Thoreau

M Y PAN AM flight landed at Miami International Airport
on March 14, 1984. My excitement and passion were
running high as I prepared to meet Richard at the
airport. As planned, he was there patiently waiting for me to
deplane. My heart was pounding as I stepped out into this new
world called America. The weather was, of course, warmer than in
the United Kingdom. As we drove away from the airport, I looked
up and saw the largest American flag I had ever seen. I couldn't
believe that after all I had been through I was finally in Richard's
convertible enjoying the breezes that set the flag—and my heart—
aflutter.

Richard was playing Jimmy Buffet, one of his favorite singers,
and he mentioned something about the Keys. I didn't know what
he was talking about. "Is that something edible?" I asked. He
started laughing, and then he explained that what the Keys were
and that he had always dreamt of living there with his forty-five-
foot Chou Lee sailboat. He loved the ocean, and enjoyed just
sitting on the shore for hours with a drink and a cigarette in his
hand, letting his imagination take him all around the world. He

loved to fish and navigate and later on he worked in many countries around the world.

As we drove towards the Keys, we stopped several times by the roadside. Once, Richard picked some daisies and placed them in my hair. He was very romantic, and proud to be with a woman eighteen years his junior. When we came to Key Largo, storm clouds gathered over us. Suddenly, it started to rain, and a few seconds later we drove out of the rain.

I suddenly remembered something that my father had said to me when I was only seven years old, and had started crying. "You know there is a place called America," he said. "It is a very faraway land and in that country there is a place where it rains on one road but not on the other, as if the neighborhood women are holding a sheet over that side of the road to keep it dry." I believe my father had a premonition that his little girl would one day live in that land.

The first week, Richard took me all around Florida, including Orlando and Disney World. I had my first experience of eating catfish, too. I was very skeptical about eating cat, because I told him that in Lebanon we don't eat cat. He finally convinced me that catfish was not a cat!

I immediately liked the Florida climate, but was waiting for some seasonal change. When I overheard other people's conversations, they always talked about the weather. So surprisingly I asked Richard, "When is it going to be cold or snow in the Keys?"

With those inquiries, Richard felt it was time to take me to the local library and start educating me about the environment and culture of the Keys. I loved the sun, the blue skies, and the turquoise water, and enjoyed the lazy days, but in the back of my mind there was a huge problem that was not going away, which was affecting my thoughts and feelings: I missed my family. During the day, I would laugh, smile, and carry on as if everything was normal, but at night I would cry my heart out. The majority of the time, I was hiding my tears and feelings. My mind was filled with thoughts and questions, such as: "Will I see my parents again? Shall I go back to Lebanon?" A war was going on inside me.

At the same time, this war provoked questions about my relationship to Richard. I was aware that sometimes women fall in love with a man's potential. Had that happened to me? Did I really love this man or had I simply wanted to leave the horrible situation in Lebanon? These questions kept buzzing around in my brain, but I couldn't come up with any answers. My friends and family expressed their disapproval, telling me that I was wasting my time with Richard.

Not long after settling in the Keys with Richard, I started to see the real man behind the friendly, loving façade. He was a very jealous man. His possessiveness made him jealous of everyone. He would instruct me not to talk to neighbors, to strangers, to anyone. I couldn't comprehend this attitude, as I had come from a small village where we were all like one big family. We talked, danced, ate, drank, played, and worked together, helping each other during harvest time, being there for one another when any one of us was feeling down or sick.

I felt lonely all the time. Here I was in the land of my dreams, and yet I withdrew from everyone. I ignored my own well-being and slipped into a state of imbalance. I blamed my partner, my parents, and my circumstances, as we all do inevitably in one way or another. Days and months passed in which I was in a state of confusion, not knowing where I stood, whether I would go back to Lebanon, or what my future would be. Some nights I would wake up and ask Richard, "When are we going to go to work? What are our plans? What's going to happen? Where we are going to end up?"

All these questions in my mind were driving me crazy, but I knew that I didn't want to go back to Beirut. That part of my life was over for me. I needed to move forward. Even when the embassy called and told me that my job was still open and that they wanted me to come back; I told them I was not returning to Lebanon. I felt that I was responsible for my life that I needed to make something out of myself.

Then, one day, I was in a dead serious mood. I let Richard know that we needed to contact his family and see if his boss wanted him for a new assignment. He listened to me, contacted his family, and luckily they had a project for him in Korea. Finally, Richard decided that he would take the job with the United States 8th Army Garrison in Youngsan, South Korea. I would stay at a friend's house until he sent me word to join him there.

9

Depression, Despair & Discovery

I am still not all I should be,
But I am bringing all my energies
To bear on this one thing:
Forgetting the past and looking forward
To what lies ahead.

Philippians 3:13

I T WAS AUGUST when Richard left for Korea for a telecommunication engineering project with the U. S. military. Every day while he was in Korea, I received a letter and a tape telling me how much he missed me and loved me, that he was preparing a place for us to live and spend a happy life together. I couldn't wait for him to put his arms around me, but my love for him was different than my love for Bernard, and Richard sensed this. I knew he could see it in my eyes.

The time came for me to go to Korea. On that day, I received another tape from Richard telling me that he had had a vasectomy. I really did not know what that was. I wanted to have a child with him. I wanted to be a mother like other women. I didn't know that a vasectomy would prevent that from happening, at least with Richard.

I left for Korea and the first couple of months were great. We had our own driver, as well as a maid. I was like a queen. But something was missing. I told Richard that we needed to get married. Suddenly, he turned sour. Our happy days came to a quick halt. Nevertheless, I prepared my paperwork by following Korean law, and went to the Lebanese Embassy in Japan to secure a letter from the ambassador there for me to marry Richard.

We were married in January, and that's when the real unhappiness set in. I didn't know what was going on with me. I knew something was happening with my health. I believed that I was depressed, and I knew that I felt unwanted. Was I really a burden to this man who didn't want to have children or a wife? All I wanted was to have a child. Was that too much to ask of him?

After a couple of years of this, I was exhausted. Depression enveloped me. Outwardly, no one knew. I had everything that a woman could want: a man who made lots of money and held a position equivalent to that of a brigadier general. We attended parties, dined with generals, and lived in a penthouse overlooking the Hon River. Yet I was miserable. I pretended that I was happy, but deep inside, the real Lela was chagrined and woefully disappointed.

Richard's true self had been hidden under a thin veneer. He became more and more controlling, possessive, domineering. He was like a dictator. He ordered me where to go and what to do and what to wear. It was like he had a split personality. He would lavish me with gifts, take me to Hawaii, Hong Kong, Singapore, Malaysia, and Thailand, but when we were going out, he would show his jealousy and insecurity.

I was petite, beautiful, and smart. I dressed fashionably, spoke intelligently, and conducted myself properly in the high-class company we kept. Why was he jealous? I didn't embarrass him by flirting with other men. I was my genuine friendly self, but he misconstrued that to satisfy the deception that played out in his mind.

By this time, I had my U. S. citizenship and was working with nineteen officers, enjoying great success and popularity. I was jovial, in great shape, and worked very hard. I became fluent in Korean and taught English as a second language to the military wives at the Korean General Headquarters. But all I had in my life was working and shopping. I became addicted to shopping, because I was searching for something that would make me happy, that would fill the huge void I felt in my life. I let outward events and other people dictate how I should feel and how I should act.

At this time in my life I started keeping journals because there was no one around me with whom I could share my feelings of loneliness and fear of dying before I saw my family again. However, I was so used to doing things that others wanted me to do and being who others wanted me to be that I couldn't be honest even with myself in my journals. When I came to look back on those scraps of diaries years later, I saw that they reflected a young woman struggling to find her place in the world but unable to truly see her situation, deal with her pain, or take responsibility for her life.

I decided that if I had to spend two years working and living in Korea, I needed to make my life as comfortable and enjoyable as I could. Living in a nice neighborhood meant that I had high-class Korean neighbors, so I made Korean friends. I carried an English-Korean dictionary and a notebook around with me, and wrote down in Korean every sentence that would help me through my daily life, whether I was shopping downtown or working in my office at the army garrison. My attitude was, "If they can speak it, so can I." Learning the language gave me the ability to move around easily in that distant land. It reminded me of my dear father, an illiterate, who once told me that the number of languages we have in our mouth tells how many persons we are.

Despite every effort to offset my unhappiness, however, I was planting unhappy thoughts in my mind every day. They pressed on my subconscious, making me feel sad and causing manifestations in my physical body. I developed thyroid disease, and felt miserable.

Nothing had meaning. Nothing had taste. Nothing felt good or beautiful. I entertained suicidal feelings, as the world seemed darker and darker to me. I knew that I had a problem and needed to turn around both my health and my attitude. There was nowhere to look but within. When all hope seemed lost, when there was no family around me, when my husband left me for temporary duty every month, I had no one to befriend but God. I wanted happiness so much that I used to beg God to come into my heart and save me from my thoughts and feelings.

In 1987, Richard was transferred to Japan, and I had to follow him. Here again, we were like vagabonds. Since I lacked human attachments, I had become attached to things that I had acquired in Korea. Now, however, everything that we had accumulated we had to either give away or sell for practically nothing to move to another country.

Once we settled in Japan, I initially worked with Richard's company. It didn't take long for me to find out that I couldn't tolerate working with him in the same office, so I applied for a job with the United States Air Force in Japan.

I spent my free time in the International Woman's Club and library. I thought if I kept myself busy, studied, and read, it would help me move forward. I taught English as a second language to a group of Japanese women, which made my life easier, healthier, and more joyful. I planned trips and parties for them and had a fascinating time. I also became fluent in Japanese, which helped me enjoy their company more.

By then, I knew that Richard was not the right man for me. I realized that I wasn't really in a relationship with him; I was working on a project. I wasn't involved with a man; I was dedicated to cause. I was not in love with Richard, but only with his potential. This has proven to be a pattern in my life. I have always chosen men who needed fixing in a particular area of their life. Some needed to open up emotionally. Others needed to heal the pain of a difficult childhood or a bad marriage. So I came to the rescue. I would offer them direction and advice to sort out their confusion, although at the same time I was confused, myself. I knew I had to make a decision about where to go from here. I wanted to stay in Japan, but would I be able to take care of myself?

Ultimately, I returned with Richard to the Florida Keys in 1989, where we purchased a little getaway cottage. After remodeling it and making it comfortable for us, I felt the need to reconnect with my family. I hadn't seen my parents since 1984. I was thirty-two years old and active, but also sad, depressed, and lonely. My relationship with Richard was continuing to deteriorate.

I purchased a ticket and left for Lebanon. Richard drove me to the airport. My thoughts and emotions were so mixed, and my feelings toward Richard so negative, that it seemed like the longest journey I had ever taken. Several years after we divorced, Richard confessed that when he was returning home from the airport that day, he found himself sobbing, thinking that I would never return and he would never see me again.

My mother lifting her hands in praise to God

And so, in 1990, with the horrible war in Lebanon led by the terrifying Michel Aoun raging, I landed in Damascus as an American citizen. My brother and one of his Muslim friends picked me up at the airport. When I stepped out of Customs after being thoroughly investigated by the Syrian officers, I saw a hand waving and heard someone calling, "Lela! Lela!" That was my name, but I didn't recognize the person approaching me. I was hesitant, and a bit frightened. Moments later, I felt a hand on my shoulder. It was my brother, whom I had not seen in twelve years. He was young and strong and happy with eyes brimming with tears. As he hugged me, I felt a tremendous feeling of relief.

As we drove towards Anjar, I was self-conscious of the fact that I was also carrying an American passport, which was not exactly the best type of identification to have in those terrible days. As an American, I was not allowed to enter Lebanon, so I was careful to hide my passport underneath my outer clothing. The Syrian Customs officer failed to find it, however, so I managed to cross the border without incident. We drove for another forty-five minutes, passing the Syrian-Israeli border in the Bekaa Valley. Finally, we arrived at the humble home of my father and mother. I looked around and saw my entire clan – my entire family, including my sisters and their children, neighbors, and friends. The whole neighborhood turned out to greet me!

As a welcome, they slaughtered a lamb and poured flowers and rice over me, just as if I was getting married. What a joyous time! My outward joy masked the sadness within me, however, and soon I felt lonely again, because I had neither a husband with me nor did I have a child to show to my family and neighbors. In my culture, these are the yardsticks of happiness. You get married. You have children. You are happy. I loved children and dearly wanted to have them, but Richard did not.

I spent my first few days recovering from jet lag. I found a little corner of the house in which to sleep, and started feeling at home again. People came day and night with bouquets of flowers, trays of baklava, and candy. They all wanted to see me. They all said that I hadn't changed at all, that I was the same petite, athletic, beautiful woman as before. I hadn't dyed my hair blonde, nor did I speak English or use English words mingled with our Anjarian dialect. They voiced pride in the fact that I had retained my cultural upbringing.

The first week, I lost my voice from talking so much, and had a hard time swallowing. Tears constantly filled my eyes. Soon, I started going out and walking around the village. I saw hundreds of Armenian families that had fled from Beirut to Anjar, fearful of bombs and rockets. My parents opened their doors to an Armenian family and gave them shelter, warm blankets, and whatever else they had to share. My sisters had left their homes, too, and found shelter at my parents' house. Anjar was safer than Beirut.

One day, I walked to my sister Mary's house. She knew how much I loved her green bean dish, and so she invited me for lunch. After we had eaten, I met a young man who was the closest friend of my nephew, Boghos (Paul). This young man, named Vatche, was very jovial, yet also arrogant. I didn't believe everything he was saying. I asked Boghos about him later, and he reminded me that I had been Vatche's Scout leader years earlier (he was ten years my junior). Boghos explained that Vatche was a jeweler, a very street smart young man. He had his own manufacturing business. The car he was driving gave me the impression that he was well-to-do and successful. We talked and laughed together. A couple of days later, Vatche and Boghos invited me to go on a picnic with them. I accepted and enjoyed my time with them very much. Then we took a ride around the village in Vatche's car.

Another time, I was walking around taking pictures of the village when I came across a cute, lovely little girl wearing a yellow dress. She reminded me of a beautiful canary. I asked her mother's permission to take a picture of her. She said, yes, and offered me Arabic coffee. I soon learned that she was Vatche's mother, and the little girl, his sister. I wondered if this was a mere coincidence, or God's way of putting someone in my path for a reason. Days passed, and I was getting used to being with my family and friends. Joy abounded, as did food and drinks, picnics and parties.

I stayed in Anjar for two-and-a-half months. I couldn't go to Beirut, because it was besieged and I didn't want to get into trouble there. My visit in Anjar had been wonderful, but my mind was on the United States, wondering what I would do if Richard left me. Again, my fearful thoughts started to take control of me, and I was feeling pain in my stomach as a result. As James Allen wrote, "As a man thinketh in his heart, so is he. We attract that which we want, and nothing else."

The day came for me to leave Lebanon, and my parents' home was like a funeral parlor. The talk in the street was that a big war was on the horizon. An ominous atmosphere hung over the Middle East as Saddam Hussein invaded Kuwait. We cried and cried. My eyes were so red and puffy I could barely see.

I returned to the same mundane routine in the Keys. Then, around one September evening in 1990, I received a telephone call from a young man calling me "Aunt." I didn't recognize his voice. He said he was calling from Canada. To my surprise, it was Vatche. Richard immediately became suspicious of my talking to this young man.

A couple of months later, Richard took a job in Guyana, South America. He said that I couldn't come with him because employees weren't allowed to bring their wives with him. We were separated for a year. I needed a job to keep busy, and was hired by the fire marshal's office. I also enrolled in the local community college to work toward a degree that would help me get a better job.

Life was again very lonely. Desert Storm was going on, and I had a difficult time concentrating on my job, since I was thinking constantly about my family. I was having problems sleeping, and all my prayers were not helping me. I managed to keep occupied with work and school, and that helped me pass the time. Deep inside, I felt the day was coming for me to end my marriage to Richard. It would take almost two more years for that to happen.

For the first couple of months that Richard was in Guyana, he would call me at least once a day and ask how I was. He told me about his work and life in South America. Soon after that, I sensed that he was not himself. He didn't sound real to me; he would become angry all of a sudden in our conversations. Although I wanted to visit him in Guyana, he didn't want me to. We made arrangements to meet in Barbados for New Year's 1992. It turned out to be the unhappiest, most miserable and most abusive time I ever had with him. He got so drunk that he started pulling my hair. I could not believe how a man could turn from a lover into a wicked man.

After that, he came back to the Keys about once every three months. Whenever he came to the States, however, he would ask me where he could buy lingerie and perfume. He said it was for his maid. When he was on the phone with me from Guyana, I knew intuitively that he was involved with another woman. Finally, in 1993, I told him that I was coming to Guyana and that he should get ready to pick me up at the Guyana Airport. He was angry, but when I landed, he came with his driver to pick me up. He was so drunk and obnoxious, I was actually afraid of him and what he might do to me.

I was on a mission to find out the truth of what was going on. When he took me to a hotel, I asked him why he wasn't taking me to his house. He didn't like my questioning him, and became abusive, pulling my hair, jumping on my small body, and flicking cigarette ashes in my eyes. I managed to free myself from his clutches and escape. I rushed to the front desk of the hotel and called security at the American Embassy. They told me that I shouldn't remain there, but instead should go to a hotel where American Embassy personnel stayed.

In a couple of hours, security arrived. They took me to a five-star hotel and sheltered me until I could find a way to leave Guyana. Meanwhile the embassy did its job locating Richard and reporting him to his company president. They told me that since Richard and I were both Americans, and husband and wife, we effectively had only two choices: to either stay together or leave together.

After that, I went with Richard to the Guyanese police station. They asked me if I wanted to press charges against him. I agreed not to press charges. In return, Richard took me to the compound where all the engineers lived. I saw immediately that all the engineers had their wives with them, and some of them had Guyanese girlfriends. Some of the people in the compound were surprised when I introduced myself as Richard's wife. Finally, I got a call at my hotel from a woman who said she was Mrs. Richard Allen. "That's impossible," I said. "I'm Mrs. Richard Allen." She said that she was married to Richard and that I had better leave the country immediately if I knew what was good for me.

The ten days that I stayed in the British Guyana jungle were a nightmare. Richard could have killed me and thrown me into the underbrush, and no one would have ever found me. In fact, he mentioned doing this in one of our conversations. By then, I would have done anything to bring him back to the United States and divorce him. Eventually, I spoke to Richard's boss, who managed to deport him to the United States.

We both returned to the Keys, and that year I received my divorce and started living the single life again. After my divorce from Richard, I continued my schooling and graduated in 1994 with an Associate degree. I received my real estate license at the same time and landed a beautiful job with the Monroe County Marathon Airport, which I managed for the FAA for almost four-and-a-half years. I was very much appreciated, in part due to my eight years' experience with the military in Korea and Japan. I was well disciplined in my work. My English had improved over the years, again as a result of my work with the U.S. Department of Defense overseas.

I had no problem finding top-paying jobs, but I kept wondering why I attracted people who were not in alignment with my dream and life goal of having a family and living a peaceful life. I kept dreaming and visualizing that one day I would meet a man who would love me as I was and for what I wanted out of life.

In the meantime, my nephew Boghos kept nudging me to visit his friend Vatche in Canada, but I was not comfortable about opening such a door at that time. A couple of years passed, and finally Vatche contacted me again. We talked extensively, and I felt that he was attracted to me. He sounded very mature and caring. This time, I was excited to see him, so when his birthday approached, I flew to Canada to visit him.

10

More Trouble in Paradise

Every human being who does any damage
Or inflicts any pain on anybody else is a far
Greater victim than [the one] he victimizes and
Must answer for all of those things
To a law of the universe.

Dr. Wayne Dyer

I FELL MADLY in lust with Vatche. It's easier to be truthful about it in hindsight, but back then, in 1993, I thought it was love. I was thirty-six, and he was just twenty-six. I brought him to the U.S., and for ten years I lived a fantasy of being married to him, but his plans were quite different than mine.

In all honesty, his agenda was not entirely his own. Vatche was a Mama's boy. His mother's agenda greatly influenced his drive to get what he wanted out of life...and out of me. I had no way of knowing, of course, because he was a very secretive person. He liked to keep everything to himself until the last minute when he completed a project, and then he would tell me about it. The first time I met Vatche, I knew that he was hiding something from me. My inner voice, my intuition told me loudly and clearly that something was not right, but I chose to ignore it and proceed to do things my way instead of God's way. I ignored the Truth, which is love's doorway.

A woman doesn't marry just a man. She marries into his family; she takes his name (unless she is more liberated and keeps her own family name). It's therefore vitally important, for the success of her marriage, to look at her fiancé's family, check out its strengths and weaknesses, and try to determine if there is a controlling influence over her fiancé from anyone in the family. I liked the idea that Vatche loved his family as much as I loved mine. What I was yet to discover, however, was that in his approach to family and business he was controlling and domineering; it was his way or the highway. Usually when he mixed business with family, the worse the situation became.

I always saw the positive in people, and Vatche saw the negative. He could not imagine getting along harmoniously with people and not controlling other people's lives. That's why we used to quarrel all the time until there was no communication left between us. In fact, Vatche's controlling attitude was his most prominent trait. He was not happy if things did not go his way. He loved business and finance, especially when dealing with his friends. He preferred working with others, rather than on his own, and was great at delegating most of the work so he could feel like a king.

Vatche was very diplomatic and convincing; to some he might even have been considered a con artist. He was certainly a wheeler–dealer. He managed to achieve success without any formal education. He had a mind that quickly evaluated everything, but didn't hold onto one idea or project too long. He always had more than one project or activity going at the same time. He was great at multi-tasking. Early on, I thought he had it all.

We did share some characteristics. We approached life with enthusiasm. We thought outside the box and had a go-getter attitude. Although I was ten years older than Vatche, he seemed like the elder, and I didn't act my age when I was around him. We shared the same mannerisms and animated quality in our conversation, and appeared to be alike in age as well. Vatche knew me like an open book; he knew my thoughts and feelings before I verbally expressed them. I, on the other hand, couldn't read him or penetrate his thoughts. Moreover, our thoughts were very different and we differed in what we wanted in life.

In the beginning, the fact that he was a jeweler by profession strongly attracted me. I fell in love with the idea of opening jewelry stores, growing our business bigger and bigger, achieving financial security, and having a family. Once again, I fell in love with a man's *potential*. As before, my habit of coming to the aid of men and trying to make the relationship work as a romance came into play. Vatche wanted his future to be safe and secure, but his strategy for this was to grow his business in the U.S. and then take everything back to Lebanon. I didn't foresee how fixated on this idea he would be, or how he would use me as a vehicle for his success.

The first year after Vatche and I got married in 1994 we were preoccupied with getting used to living together in the Florida Keys. Vatche had to wait for his paperwork from Immigration before he could start a job. I was the breadwinner of the household, and we were barely making it on my $1,200 a month.

I always wanted children, and finally, at age thirty-eight, I got pregnant. When the news broke, however, Vatche was not happy at all. He wanted me to have the child aborted because of our economic situation. He said that he couldn't take care of a child, that he didn't want it to go through poverty like he did, and that he wasn't ready to be a father.

Being pregnant and at the same time worrying about our financial situation was very stressful. I felt sick every day. One day, I got out of bed feeling weak, and fainted. Vatche took me to Miami, and the abortion was done the same day. I really had no voice in the decision or, rather, I abdicated my choice out of fear. I thought that Vatche would leave me if I had the child. Neither Vatche's family nor mine was aware of these circumstances; they were not even aware that we were married.

After he acquired his U.S. citizenship, Vatche acted very differently around me. We barely communicated. I wanted to believe that he loved me, because we had been strongly attracted to one another, but in the back of my mind, I wasn't comfortable with his thoughts, emotions, and actions. He was a very deceptive person. In truth, we were not in sync, and no matter how much I wanted to believe that we would survive as a couple, the cards to the contrary had already been dealt.

For years, I tried to convince Vatche to do simple things with me, like attending my business banquets, weddings, christenings, or just going out with friends, but he wouldn't. Nor did he want to have children, raise a family, or have a beautiful home with me where our families could come and share our life. I became pregnant a second time at age forty and aborted again because Vatche didn't want to be a father. I knew that was a sin, and for those sins I endured considerable pain and guilt for many years. After I realized what was going on, I could have left Vatche, but I didn't. I realized what was going on about two or three years into the marriage, but I stayed in the marriage for another seven years.

I lived with anger toward Vatche for the last ten years that I was married to him. When he started to become successful in his jewelry business and I started making money in real estate, I used to tell him, "If you couldn't have a child with me, at least let's have a beautiful house where we can live together," but he didn't want that either. All he wanted was to grow his business and then go back to Lebanon and buy land there.

Every two or three months he returned to Lebanon. He was buying land and building houses there, but he never told me anything about his activities. He was taking everything that we had and putting it into Lebanon, so that when he was ready to leave, he could just say to me, "I'm going back. If you want to come, you can come." His attitude was that when he was back in Lebanon, he would be able to live like a king. His entire course of action was premeditated.

The truth was that I allowed Vatche to intimidate me, so much so that I wasn't honest with my own family. Once, when I visited my parents in Lebanon, they looked me in the eyes and asked me why I didn't have children. Instead of telling them the truth, I lied and said that I didn't want children.

Vatche, for his part, had not been truthful to his own parents, and had not told them that I was his legal wife. In my culture, it is considered immoral to have a child out of wedlock, so by lying to his family about our marital state, he was able to explain our lack of children. I didn't realize how much this prejudiced me in the eyes of his family, until one day his mother came up to me and upbraided me for preventing her son from having a family. "Don't I deserve to have the fruits of my son?" she demanded. "Don't I deserve to be a grandmother?" I was too ashamed to tell her that the decision to remain childless was her son's, and not mine.

Following this encounter, I went to the bathroom and cried my heart out. I knew that the Good Lord had a plan for me. I asked continuously in my prayers for forgiveness and for God to show me the way out of these miserable feelings. I heard His voice in Galatians 4:27: "Be glad, O barren woman, who bears no children; break forth and cry aloud, you who have no labor pains; because more are the children of the desolate woman than of her who has a husband."

Vatche and I were no longer in harmony with one another. Year by year we fell more out of love and shared fewer and fewer interests. He wanted nothing to do with living a normal life in the United States. His thoughts, energy, feelings, dreams, projects, and life were in Lebanon, but he needed to make the money here first. Over the years, his family played many tricks on me behind my back. Because they didn't know I was his legal wife in the United States, they didn't treat me with the respect I was due. I was hurt when I realized the truth. This impacted my behavior so much that I started feeling hateful and resentful towards his family.

I gave up most of my friends and neighbors in favor of Vatche's priorities, and each time I gave up something in hopes of winning his approval I relinquished a piece of myself in the process. The more I sacrificed, the less remained of me until one day I woke up feeling empty. I felt that I had lost my womanhood and femininity. Being a workaholic allowed me to bury my feelings of neglect on the part of Vatche and his family, which I grew to resent. I became overwhelmed with anxiety and depression, and I suffered enormous loss of self-esteem. All these negative feelings were again affecting me physically; I gained weight, and felt like a balloon being inflated to the point of bursting.

As I look back, there had been warning signs, but I ignored them. Vatche was too closely tied to his family members. He seemed to talk to, consult with, and confide in them to an abnormal extent. The result was that I felt like an outsider, excluded from his family. He refused to take my side in family arguments. Another sign was that he liked to be in charge. He always made a strong impression, knew what he wanted, never showed fear, and always insisted on his own way. Eventually, however, I realized that he had to be in control at all times. At first, I felt that he was taking care of me, but in the end I felt that I was living with a dictator.

During these years of struggle and heartache, my family was far away geographically, but my niece Yeva and my brother Khatchig heard my cries half a world away, consoled me, and shared my rare moments of laughter and joy. Yeva was my accountability partner. She allowed me to talk about my problems. Although she was on the other side of the globe, I could visualize her nodding her head as I talked. These conversations lasted for a year, but I recognized that my family's support was not an ultimate solution to the problem. I needed to alter my thought processes and adjust my entire outlook. I prayed to God to acquire more tolerance and understanding.

Finally, I invited Vatche's mother and sister to lunch in my humble little cottage in the Florida Keys. My words to them that day came from my heart. They cried as I related stories of my life with their son and brother. They were surprised at how well I handled myself under those circumstances in which they had been deceptive and secretive toward me. When I finally leveled with Vatche's family, I felt free. The truth, as the saying goes, set me free. I learned that it is better to let go and be truthful than to hold grudges or negative thoughts, because they have a way of coming back and haunting you.

I was hiding behind a mask, and years of wearing this mask took a heavy toll on me. As a result, I carried the burden of sadness, torment, and chagrin. I stayed sad, angry, and unhappy, blaming myself for what happened to me for almost two decades, just because I let my emotions control me. I was not true to my feelings; I covered them with a mask not showing my true self. This hurt me not only physically, emotionally, and mentally; it also hurt those who came into contact with me. The bitterness killed my beauty and marred my feelings toward others.

The breakdown of communication often generates heartbreak and disappointment concerning unfulfilled dreams, visions, and goals. I had always envisioned a lovely family home with a child and friends for myself. I held onto this vision, but unfortunately Vatche wanted something different. The time finally came when I couldn't stand being his presence.

From L to R: My father, my mother, and my brother-in-law (2001)

My mother once told me, "If you don't trust someone, stop and pull out of the situation you are in with that person, because true love is not an emotional risk. The real risk is marrying a person because it is convenient. If you hurt yourself emotionally, you're creating painful experiences, building walls around you." When there was no possibility of making things better between Vatche and myself, I had no choice but to end our relationship. Thank God, I chose life. "Resist the devil and it will flee." I became the victor, instead of the victim.

I needed to make a quick decision, because I knew that Vatche would make a run for it when the time came. He was already giving out signals; he had closed both his stores in the Keys and was preparing to move back to Lebanon. What was I going to do? What was going to happen? What consequences would I face as a result of my divorce from him? Finally, I became serious about my decision to draw the line, set my own boundaries, move ahead, and leave the miserable life I had with him. It wasn't easy to tell him, and when I did, I was surprised that he didn't take me seriously.

I learned from this that nobody should allow himself or herself to remain under the control of another. Eleanor Roosevelt said, "No one can make you feel inferior without your consent." After ten years of marriage, I realized that I had been seriously mistaken. I had fallen in love for the wrong reason again. Now, when I look back at those years with Vatche, I laugh and wonder why I stayed with him so long.

Thomas Edison once said, "I have not failed; I have just found ten thousand ways that do not work." I realize now that I was not a failure in my life journey. From this failed relationship I learned to value life, to have integrity, to think positively, and to maintain a positive self-image.

After a while, whenever I saw Vatche in our community in the Florida Keys, I felt nothing. I had turned the corner, but I still needed time to grieve over my loss before I could fully recover and transform myself.

11

Dealing with Loss

Life is a series of experiences, each one
Of which makes us bigger, even though
It is hard to realize this. For the world was
Built to develop character, and we must learn
That the setbacks and griefs which we
Endure help us in our marching forward.

Henry Ford
1863-1947

LOSS CAN CARVE a crater in your soul, and just as quickly replace it with an equal amount of joy. Consider the family that loses a loved one only to have a baby born into the family soon afterward, or the family that loses its homeland only to find greater happiness in a new country. We lose loved ones through many different circumstances, including long separation, divorce, and death. Regardless, loss is a painful setback.

Divorce is a "living death." It's worse than knowing your spouse is dying. Going through a divorce can take a long time and involve haunting memories, unresolved issues, unsolved mysteries, and denial. I had been through divorce before, and felt I was fully prepared for my second one. Still, no matter how much I tried to view this change in a positive light, I blamed myself, called myself every name in the book, berated myself for being stupid, felt guilty, and even called myself crazy. Fortunately, I eventually realized that negative thinking and feeling guilty was not going to help me one bit.

Luckily, in the throes of my divorce, my family and friends were there to encourage me to see the brighter side of life. I owe a great debt of gratitude to those who stood by me day and night, supporting me, and encouraging me to think positively and take positive actions. Even at times when I thought I was losing everything, I was sure of one thing—that God loved me, was there for me, would provide for me, and would heal my wounds. I found something within me that was greater than my problems and greater than my loss. I started laughing at my mistakes, forgiving myself, and forgiving others. I thanked my enemies for what they had done, and took full responsibility for life and my feelings.

Our perception makes a big difference in how we recover from a loss, and how long that recovery takes. It was painful to let go of my relationship, but when I did, my life was actually less stressful because I was freed from the burdens and responsibilities from which I had previously suffered. I encouraged and inspired myself with the knowledge that my circumstances would change, and that I would feel better after my grieving ended. I was able to turn my energy toward being productive in my profession, which satisfied me by helping other people. I learned that losing a partner through divorce was not the end of my life. How I perceived my loss was crucial to determining my future and how I would move forward with my life. It was all up to me to decide when I would stand up, pick up the pieces, and move on.

It took two years for me to grieve over my loss. I gave permission to do that, but also I put a time limit on my grieving and to cease thinking and talking about Vatche. At times during this period, I withdrew from family, friends, neighbors, and co-workers in order to have a conversation with myself. I looked closely within myself for that innocent little girl I had once been. I started going to the gym, stopped smoking, and even gave up my two daily glasses of wine. I found peace, love, joy, and laughter. People started to enjoy being around me again, and I began to attract people who shared my outlook on life and business. I realized that I had to first learn to love myself before I could love others.

One day, I cleaned out all my love letters from Vatche, along with my photo albums of him. I burned all of them and threw them to the winds. Once I did that, I felt free of blame, guilt, resentment, and pain. For ten to fifteen minutes a day, I sought out a clean, well-lit place where I could retreat and carry on a conversation with the spirit within me. These conversations helped me to come to terms with my loss and the harmful effects that I suffered emotionally, mentally, and physically.

We make poor choices; this is human nature. But we are all here on Earth for a reason. We can all turn our life around by raising our awareness, increasing our knowledge, recognizing our opportunities, and understanding our challenges. We can forgive ourselves for our mistakes and others for the pain they have inflicted on us, and then move on with our life with an open mind and heart. People ask me if I could love again, and I tell them, "Absolutely!" I love helping people who are going through difficult times. I love giving companionship to elderly people and lending an empathetic ear to those less fortunate than I. Isn't that love?

My failure to bear children has also been a major loss in my life. Little girls grow up believing that they will marry and have children. It seems to be the primary validation of their gender. For those women who cannot bear children or who have chosen not to, there remains a void that must be filled in some other way.

The law of cause and effect had a lot to do with my not having had children. Every cause has its effect; nothing happens by chance alone. I got into my marriage to Vatche without looking at what kind of a man he was within, without getting to know his true values as a human being, his beliefs, or his emotions. I failed to observe how he dealt with his family, friends, and strangers. I lied not only to myself, but to my family as well. Whatever happened to me was a result of what I attracted to myself.

Finally, in 1997, I decided I needed a spiritual facelift to remove old emotional scars. Nobody could help me do this; I had to go it alone. I did a visualization and imagination exercise to cleanse my soul from within. I visualized a refrigerator in which the bottom compartments were filled with fruits and vegetables that had not been touched for months. What happens in such a case? The rotten potatoes will spoil the apples, and so the bitterness and poison will be passed to all the other food in the compartment. In my imagination, I started by cleaning the bottom drawer of rotten fruit one at a time. I looked to the future with expectation of moving forward, onward, and upward. I could have had a child by birth or adoption; but I didn't have the right partner to share in my child's life. I wanted my child or children to have an earthly father. I knew that I wasn't going to be a successful single mother; that's why I chose not to be one at all.

I learned that if I was battling bitterness or weakness of any kind, the enemy was intent on keeping me from walking by faith. The enemy would try to keep me in an emotional state, controlled by my weaknesses. By practicing faith, I got up on my feet every time my life was tossed around by situations or circumstances. How many of us praise God when everything is plentiful and prosperous, and then blame God when things don't go our way? I learned to be wary of feeling sorry for myself. There is power in faith that will appear if a person lets things unfold in God's time. Everything has its time, season, and purpose. We can't force things to happen to us or to others. Instead, we have to let things happen naturally by allowing the energy to flow through us and outwardly to touch other people.

The lesson to learn is how we can rebound and reposition our lives after we've suffered a disappointment or loss. We aren't judged by how many times we've been knocked down, but by how many times we've gotten up again. If I had had children, it would have been a twenty-four-hour-a-day job. I believe now that God had other plans for me; knowing that has given me strength and courage toward fulfillment of that divine plan.

The greatest loss of all, however, is that of one's parents. My father died while I was still married to Vatche, and my mother died after my marriage to him ended. Each loss compounded the previous one, took an extra toll on me, and caused me to re-evaluate my life and goals.

The last time I saw my father was during the Christmas and New Year's holiday of 1999-2000. He was so happy to see me dressed in my Santa Claus costume for my nieces, nephews, and their children.

My father was a Psalm 128 father. He gathered his children around him, nurtured them, fed them, and protected them. I will always remember when he came home from the fields; he would have something special for me in his pocket so it wouldn't go to waste. Maybe it was the first fruit of the vineyard or some wheat seeds. He was very frugal, very careful, and very hardworking. The last thing he told me on the telephone a week before he passed away was, "Lela, take care. Don't spend all your money."

It was a hot day, August 11th, a Sunday in 2002. I was celebrating Vatche's birthday at the time. All of a sudden, I reached to my ears to check for the earrings that my father had given me. He had saved some money and bought them for me when I last saw him. At the same moment, I clearly remember reaching for the Bible, which was always on my living room table. I read Psalm 128, "Blessed are all who fear the Lord, who walk in his ways." I had dedicated this verse to my father six months previously. Intuitively, I felt something was happening to him. He was a healthy eighty-four-year-old, who had worked every day of his life, starting before dawn. The time difference between the Keys and Lebanon is seven hours, but the vibration and the law of attraction doesn't recognize geographical distance. My father and I were connected.

I kept reading and truly listening to my inner voice, and I prayed that all was well. That afternoon went well, but the following morning, August 12th, at 7:30, my telephone rang. That was very unusual, so I was startled. I hardly ever received calls at such an early hour. Knowing that all my family was in the Middle East if something were wrong, they would call me in the wee hours of the morning, and that possibility scared me to death.

I was still thinking about my intuition concerning my father the day before. All I could hear from the handset was a woman's voice telling Vatche, "He passed away." I became hysterical. I was so afraid something had happened to my one and only brother who had a wife and four siblings that I couldn't breathe. Finally, after I controlled myself, I called Lebanon. When I heard my brother's trembling voice, I was relieved. We loved our father. He was there for everyone, and he was like a friend to my brother, especially. They worked together so well in the fields and orchards.

After my father's burial, I went to Lebanon, visited his grave, and stayed in Anjar for a month mourning my father's death. All I wanted to do was put my head on my pillow and feel sorry for myself. However, my father's death raised my level of awareness. All of a sudden, I noticed that everything was in vibration. It was moving faster, and yet I wasn't moving an inch toward knowing or having what God had given me as my birthright. Everything that I noticed, felt, heard, dreamed, intuited, and remembered had meaning. Everything! I realized that there was no such thing as a random act. Everything was significant. There were no coincidences.

I intuited that my relationship with Vatche was ending. We were two people with different purposes and motives. Vatche was back in America, but his heart and mind were in Lebanon. I was in Anjar, but in my imagination, I was seeing the blue skies, turquoise water, sunrises, and sunsets of the Florida Keys.

After my father passed away, my mother was very sad, lonely, frustrated, and empty. In January 2006, I had just returned from a high school reunion in California, where I had a wonderful time with old friends. While I was there, I called my mother's home. I intuitively felt that something was going on, and that I should be there. I spoke with my mother, and could hear that her voice was feeble. I decided that nothing was more important than being with her, so I left for Lebanon right away. I found her in the hospital in a coma; I knew she had been hanging on, waiting for me to come.

After a couple of days being around her, she started coming back. She opened her eyes and recognized me. Her voice was very deep and her eyes were glassy. I stayed next to her for fifteen days, both day and night, to take care of her. I cut her hair with her permission and painted her nails to lift her spirit a bit. I wanted to do anything to put a smile on her face. She had a red shirt with her in the hospital. It was unusual for women in her culture to wear bright colors, but I promised that when she came to the U.S. she would wear that shirt.

I prayed ceaselessly that she would cross this life without pain. The last day when I was getting ready to leave Lebanon, I sat next to her on her bed. I asked her if she wanted to live. She said, "Darling, I think I am ready to move on and cross this bridge to join your father." There was so little life left in her eyes that she couldn't even cry. I told her that I loved her and if that's what she wanted, that's what she should do.

I left Lebanon in peace. During the next few weeks I called home every day. On February 17, 2006, something was different. I was in real estate training and rushed to my office to pick up the phone and speak to my brother. They told me that our mother was upstairs in her room waiting to say good-bye. Through my tears, I told him to gather all my sisters around her and hold hands. "Tell Mom that I am with her, that I love her and will miss her." I was sobbing. I could feel the moment was near. They went upstairs and did what I told them to do. I hung up the phone and continued to pray with them. In three minutes, my oldest nephew called me with the news that she had passed away with a big smile on her face.

What I took away from that experience was that when we are in alignment with those whom we love and respect, we feel their love, their happiness, their pain, and the very breaths they take. This is real! It's not a psychic feeling. It's an intuitive faculty that all of us have within us, but few of us exercise. I felt my mother communicating to me, and her message was, "You can do it all! You can have it all! You can be what you want to be and have what you want to have!"

Love makes everything meaningful. There are many different kinds and ways of loving a person. It's the greatest gift, and one that I inherited from my mother and father. It's a spiritual experience that can't be touched or seen, but can be felt. It's magical. It changes how we see ourselves and how we see the world around us. The time and place in which we experience this love becomes sacred. The person we love is sacred. This *agape*, this spiritual love, this unconditional love quenched my spirit and transformed me. I felt a love within me that I had never felt before. It was a great spiritual awakening.

I have been knocked down several times in my life. It took me years to recover from the emotional pain that I suffered from losing parents and partners, but my invincible and unwavering faith has enabled me to stand on my feet again because the experience of love transformed me and made me a new person.

12

Healing & Transformation

It really doesn't matter if the
Person who hurt you deserves
To be forgiven. Forgiveness is a
Gift you give yourself. You have
Things to do and you want to move on.

Real Life Preacher
July 7, 2003

T HE FIRST STEP in healing, especially from divorce or great disappointment involving another person, is to forgive. We need to forgive in order to heal the wounds or scars that remain from our relationships, because we no longer want to be hurt by them. Forgiveness is a vital step toward healing and moving forward. A favorite saying of mine is from the Greek sage, Epictetus: "We are disturbed not by what happens to us, but by our thoughts about what happens." These words have resonated with me ever since I first heard them.

"I can forgive, but I can't forget" is another way of saying, "I won't forgive." Forgiveness, when it is real and genuine, is like a scalpel that can remove the pus from old emotional wounds. When I learned how to forgive, let go, and let God take over my life, a new, youthful attitude and spirit erased the wrinkles from my face and put a sparkle in my eyes once again. We must learn the great law of cause and effect, action and reaction. It took me a while to learn, understand, implement, and live as the person that I am according to that law.

Asking questions aloud can give us added insight into ourselves. Sometimes we don't know what we really believe, feel, or desire, until we hear our own ideas spoken from our own mouth. I usually talk to myself and ask questions about why things are happening to me or why I'm acting the way I do.

After the death of my parents and my divorce from Vatche, I talked to myself a lot. If one builds a fire with newspaper alone, the flames quickly shoot high into the air, but just as quickly die down. The same is true with relationships that form on lust and physical attraction. They fade quickly. I realized through my discussion with myself that my relationships with men had all been ill-founded. No matter how long they lasted, they were doomed from the start.

When relationships end, the healing period may take months or years. That's the time when we need to embrace the healing power of love. This is our opportunity to surrender to the moment and detach ourselves from negative thoughts. Only by doing this can we heal our emotional pain. We need to express feelings that we have held onto so tightly. Love washes away fear, hurt, guilt, and anger. By letting go, and letting love in, we can rediscover our true self and feel purged, refreshed, and closer to our remaining loved ones,

What I have learned about healing is that we build up a great deal of resentment within ourselves, which rarely allows the healing process to work. No pharmaceutical medicine can work in such cases. Instead, we need to change our mindset with the affirmation that we are cured and happy. When this is done seriously it will cure the problem, no matter what it is. I believe that all of our physical pain comes from emotional bondage.

To achieve this mindset, we need first of all to have no resentment or ill feeling toward anyone. Virtually every human being in the world has, or has had, resentment or ill feelings toward others. To get out of this trap, we have to first think of all the people who were once the target of our ill feelings. Then we have to talk to them and tell them that we are sorry for whatever happened. By forgiving ourselves, and those who hurt us in the past, we can move into the future with a clean slate. It helps to remember the trigger incident very clearly. This has to be a very serious effort. Normally, when we truly repent, we cry. Once we have released all of our ill feelings, then our mindset will automatically change and we will be healed. When we finally relax, we will be able to laugh, and laughter is the best medicine of all.

My personal experience is that when I approach my goals with seriousness, I get what I want, but when I'm not very serious things don't happen. Every time that life has knocked me down, I got up and moved on—even when I was alone and away from my family. In fact, not having loved ones around inspired me more, because I had to exercise more self-discipline. I don't completely forget the past, but I don't dwell on it, either. I push and move forward, because there are better things to do and the best is always yet to come.

While grieving over my divorce and the loss of my mother, I prayed that Vatche would find happiness with his newfound love and family and dedicated myself to improving my awareness and helping others who were going through similar situations. I had a friend from Spain who spent hours on the phone with me until he saw me turn the corner. He would remind me every day via e-mail to go to the gym and stay in good health, because the mind/body connection is very important. He encouraged me to choose the right thoughts, attitudes, and feelings, to exercise, eat the right kinds of foods, and stay healthy.

When we don't give ourselves time to heal, we make poor choices; then we wonder why we keep attracting the same kind of men or women into our lives. We have to ask ourselves what we really want out of life and how we can make the best and highest use of our precious assets and faculties. I spent fifteen minutes each morning doing visualization and imaginative techniques, and another fifteen minutes reading the Scripture. I was amazed at what happened. Allowing my nerves to relax enabled me to laugh again. I felt released from blame, guilt, resentment, and pain. I became energized and started looking straight at problems and challenges, believing that I could move the mountain before me with the right positive mental attitude. I discovered that if I couldn't laugh at myself, I would be less willing to take risks in my life.

Life goes on, and I wanted to do something with mine. I had been under the control of others who had thwarted my growth for too long. Now it was time to change all of that. Anaïs Nin, the famous French author, wrote, "And the day came when the risk to remain in a bud was more painful than the risk it took to blossom." There was risk in blossoming, of course, but I decided to start planning for what I wanted to accomplish in my life.

In order to heal from pain, it's necessary to find someone or something new to love. The more I saw that I had options, the better I felt. I noticed that people were looking at me and asking questions like, "What does she have that we don't have?" I knew that I was carrying true love within myself, and that it was expanding and expressing itself outwardly. Once I started healing, doing, and being who I wanted to be, family, friends, and co-workers all came together to join my victory.

I am often reminded of the time that I first crossed the Atlantic Ocean to the land discovered by Christopher Columbus—America! We are like Columbus; we are the captains of our own ship, and we have several important tools and personnel on board with us:

1. OUR WILL is the ship's rudder. It determines the direction in which the ship is sailing and our ability to focus on the desired harbor, our goal or dream. No matter what other people do or say, the challenges we meet depend on our ability to focus our attention on our goal.

2. OUR CONSCIOUS MIND is the man in the lookout post. He can only take us to a known harbor. He reacts to everything he hears, sees, smells, tastes, and touches. He follows the ocean currents and doesn't know how to go against the wind.

3. OUR SUBCONSCIOUS MIND is our first mate. He steers our ship in the direction he is told to, but he can't tell the difference between the captain's voice (ours) and the voice of the person in the lookout post. We have to constantly direct our first mate in the direction in which we wish to sail. As soon as we lose sight of our harbor or do something that takes us in the wrong direction, the first mate listens to the man in the lookout post, and then we are no longer on course.

4. OUR MEMORY is the ship's hold. There's room for everything here; our memory is perfect if we have made an effort to keep it intact. This means we have to open the hold and let the things we want to remember in.

5. OUR IMAGINATION is our harbor. It's the image of our dream or goal. Our imagination takes us beyond the horizon, just like Columbus when he sailed and found America. We need to let our imagination take us where we want to go, continually creating the hope, the burning desire to be who we want to be and giving us unwavering faith that we will realize our desires.

6. OUR PERCEPTION is the distance to our harbor, but it also makes the distance what it is. If we compare it to a much longer distance, then it becomes smaller and much easier to reach. Our perception can give us energy by making the destination seem within sight.

7. OUR INTUITION is our map. It guides us and shows us the way. It tells us how to steer the ship. We have to learn to use our intuition and not listen to our conscious mind (the man in the lookout post) except for information on where we are now. Then we have to use our will (the rudder) to keep our first mate steering our ship in the right direction.

8. OUR THOUGHT is our sail. How we think determines the way we set our sail. This brings forth action, and that action will take us to our goal. Negative thinking allows for little wind to get into the sail. With our sail set poorly, we will never arrive at our destination. Whatever we can conceive mentally, we can bring into manifestation.

James Allen said, "Calmness of mind is the jewel of wisdom." When we have this calmness, we attract people; we become a magnet for abundance, riches, loving relationships, opportunity, and success. Change is inevitable, so shifting our paradigm and seeing the good in every situation is the key to success. I advise people, no matter where they are in their careers, not to rely on just one stream of income. I'm currently not just a real estate agent, but am also an investor and a coach. Now I'm so happy and grateful that I wake up with a smile on my face every morning. My mind and heart are strong and healthy. No storm shall destroy this house in which I live. As Louisa May Alcott wrote, "I am not afraid of storms, for I am learning how to sail my ship."

13

Sowing the Seeds of Success

Believe in yourself! Have faith in
Your abilities! Without a humble
But reasonable confidence in your
Own powers, you cannot be
Successful or happy.

Rev. Norman Vincent Peale

SUCCESS COMES IN many different ways. Some people earn it through hard work, and some through education. Others simply achieve it by applying their most predominant ability or skills. The bottom line is that prosperity and success come from within not from the outside. Surefire ingredients for success include relentless commitment to one's goals, being authentic, persistence, and being willing to take risks.

Farming the land, as my father did, provides a good analogy for success in any job, business, or relationship. The farmer starts by planting healthy seeds, believing in his ability to tend to his crops, to irrigate them, and then to reap a bountiful harvest.

We, too, must start with good seeds—healthy, positive thoughts and attitude, a strong self-image, confidence, and integrity — to receive a positive result. To make these "seeds" grow success for us, we further need desire, determination, and diligence. None of these can be purchased at the local dollar store. They are inside each of us, however, and only we can tap into them to move us on our way to a life of greater abundance and happiness. We have to make a choice; it is ours for the making. Once this decision has been made, nothing can stop us!

1. Choosing to Change

We have to choose to change. Doing the same thing over and over again will yield only the same result. In his book, *The Science of Getting Rich*, Wallace D. Wattle wrote, "Getting rich is the result of doing things in a certain way."

I believe that we make our own success or failure. We have a choice to live or die, to be healthy or sick, to be happy or sad. Will we choose life and continue to press forward? The decision is up to us.

2. Attitude Adjustment

At some point in our lives, we all need an attitude adjustment. Life throws us curves and gets our attitude out of balance. We lose a job, a spouse, a home, or a country, and we react as humans do. We grumble, gripe, and, most of all, we lose sight of the value of a good attitude.

Carolyn Warner wrote these words, which have shaped my thoughts on the importance of one's attitude:

I am convinced that attitude is the key to success in almost any of life's endeavors. Your attitude—your perspective, your outlook, how you feel about yourself, how you feel about other people—determines your priorities, your actions, your values. Your attitude determines how you interact with other people and how you interact with yourself.

When we change our attitude, we change our life! In fact, the winner's image is all about attitude. We come to this way of thinking, feeling, and acting a certain way in order to unfold our true being. Our authenticity is a vital piece of the success puzzle.

It takes a strong person to leave behind the ashes of loss, disappointment, and heartache, and all the negative emotions that revolve around those life experiences. We must part company with guilt, anger, frustration, and the "get-even" mentality that so often accompanies the breakdown of partnerships, whether business or personal.

We must examine our part in the failures that we have experienced. What was our attitude at the time? How much did we contribute to our own failures? How did we feel about others involved, and how did we treat them? Would the result have been different if we had adjusted our attitude? These questions are not easy to answer, but they must be addressed in order to move on to the next stage in our journey to success. As Earl Nightingale wrote:

A great attitude does much more than to turn on the lights in the world; it seems to magically connect us to all sorts of serendipitous opportunities that were somehow absent before the change.

Note the final words of that quote: "opportunities that were somehow absent before the change." We miss opportunities for success and happiness when our attitude is in need of adjustment. When we undergo self-examination, and do so in complete honesty with ourselves, we open doors to the rich blessings of happiness and success.

My attitude and vision of what I want and where I truly want to be are much different than what I envisioned twelve years ago. By changing my attitude, I became a secretary of a U. S. Army general, an airport manager, and a successful entrepreneur, realtor, and investor. The bottom line is that we have to accept life as it comes. I turned ashes into beauty just by making small adjustments in my attitude.

I love what Dr. Wayne Dyer says about attitude: "When you change the way you look at things, the things you look at change." How true these words are!

3. Self-Image

Aldous Huxley once said, "There is only one corner of the universe you can be certain of improving, and that is your own self." Looking back on all my years of disappointments and successes, I am convinced that if I had spent the same amount of energy concentrating solely on my own self-interest instead of giving it away to others, I would have been ten times better off materially than I am today. On the other hand, because I sacrificed myself, the negative experiences I had as a result awakened me to the path of self-realization and rebirth.

Passion, which is the power within, is far greater than anything I can imagine. One must go inside and dig deep to reform, rebuild, and reconnect; this can take a long time. Going through narrow path and enduring life's ups and downs requires a brave heart. Perception is the basis of self-identity and self-esteem. It's been said only two percent of people in the world have positive self-esteem.

How others saw me didn't matter when I was growing up in Lebanon. How I saw myself did. In a place as small as Anjar, and in a country where women didn't have any voice to speak up about religion, politics, achievement, business, and rights, people looked on me as someone who didn't belong. I saw myself differently. I wanted to be heard and have a voice of my own. I acted differently and had different opinions and perceptions about religion and education. My perception of myself was for more powerful than the situation and environment in which I lived. I saw myself as a successful person from the beginning.

As I write this book, I've been in sales for twelve years. Some salespeople have low sales and are always struggling to raise them, without success. Many of these people are always broke, they never look happy, and they are always in debt. Why? It's because they are desperately trying to change their end result. The results in their lives are determined by their actions, and their actions are determined by their self-image. We need to understand that our results are a direct reflection of our self-image.

If a salesperson's self-image is dependent on his or her sales volume, they are in error. They can change their result by improving their self-image. Similarly, we can begin immediately to plant a new self-image in our subconscious mind. We are completely responsible for our circumstances. If we want to change our circumstances, we have to change our self-image, thoughts, feelings, and actions. The difference between a successful person and those who are less successful is an awareness of a certain place within themselves. It's called the higher self, and this higher self is perfection. If we want to succeed and call on our higher self, we will succeed not for ourselves alone, but for the entire universe.

4. Goal-Setting

"Success is the progressive realization of a worthy goal," Earl Nightingale has said. Our goals are always weighing heavily on us, always peering over our shoulders, adding pressure and stress when we fall short of our timetable. Then we go into crisis. This crisis is our turning point, our awakening. A turning point raises our consciousness, prompting us to ask ourselves how we got here and what we are doing.

When I finished my tour of serving the U.S. military in peacetime in Korea and Japan in 1989, I wanted to do what I always wanted to do: sell and buy properties for others and for myself. I asked Richard Allen, "Is there a way that I could become a salesperson in the United States?" He looked at me and said, "Sport, this is the land of opportunity. Ask and it shall be given unto you..." At that moment, my round eyes got wider and I shouted, "I'm in! Where do I start?"

I didn't have a clue that I would have to go to school to get a real estate license, and the first time I took the class, and would fail it. But I never gave up until I received my license. I walked, talked, and acted like a millionaire real estate agent. I always looked at my goals "as if" I had already accomplished what I wanted. I attended seminars, hired my own mentor, and worked for the most trusted company in the Florida Keys. I developed a system and became rookie of the year, and as the years progressed I continuously implemented these strategies and techniques, which brought me riches and abundance in my life.

I also was drawn to owning rental property, money lending, world travel, motivational speaking, and on and on. My specific goal was to purchase one piece of property per year until I had twenty properties by the time I turned fifty-five. I wrote this goal on a on a 3 x 5 card and carried it in my pocket for years. I also specified what I would do to get where I wanted to be. I held onto that goal with faith until I was touching it with my hand and seeing it with my eyes. I studied this concept for years, and incorporated it into my real estate business and investments.

5. Write it down!
When I was still in secondary school at the Evangelical school in Anjar, an Armenian minister, the Reverend Jack Jambazian, visited us from California. He taught me to jot down my thoughts and prepare a "to do" list, noting everything that I wanted to do. This helped me prioritize my work and get a lot more done. I owe a lot of my success in life to this minister. We all fantasize one way or

another. By putting our dreams and goals in writing we can help to make them more concrete. We can specify what, when, and how we're going to undertake the process of getting where we are headed, what we need to do, what specific time we plan to achieve that goal, what we are willing to do and sacrifice for it, and why it is important to us.

Even now, I make sure to write down six things before going to bed that I want to accomplish the following day. The principle behind this is that when we write down our desires, needs, concerns, and worries and put that list by our bedside, our subconscious mind, which never sleeps, goes to work for us and starts solving any problems on the list.

6. Attracting What We Need to Grow

That which we desire, we attract. Understanding and practicing the law of attraction has been one of the key elements of my success. To desire is to expect, and to expect is to achieve. When we fully realize that thought causes everything, our life changes spiritually, emotionally, and financially. Nothing happens by accident or chance. It happens by design, discipline, and positive attitude. All we need to do in order to tap into this invisible power is to align ourselves with what we desire.

We can't desire that which doesn't exist. It's like imagining we're on an open fishing boat in the middle of the ocean. The sun is hot. We're enjoying the day. Our purpose for being on the ocean is to have fun and catch some fish. When we're casting our line, we're expecting that we will catch a big fish. We have to be in alignment with the idea of catching that fish, attracting it to our bait. It will jerk us around for a moment, and we will feel the excitement, but if we don't reel it in, we won't be able to keep that fish.

Desiring without expectation that we will get what we desire is like idle wishing or daydreaming. We have to have a backbone, not a wishbone. Wishful thinking and prayer will get us nowhere. We need to get up from our chair and move our legs one step at a time to get closer to our goal. Quite often we concentrate on the past more than we live in the present. The past is the past. We have to let the dead bury the dead, and start working on what we want to attract. We need to expect that we will succeed and allow it to come to us.

It helps to remove ourselves from reasoning and to disbelieve what our mind tells us. Where there is only reasoning, there is no faith. Where there is faith, there is hope, and when we have hope of getting what we desire in life, we will achieve it. We need to seek, study, learn, and meditate on the secret law of mental creation. Nature doesn't deprive us; rather, it provides us with all that is essential and good for us. We need only form a clear mental picture of what we want, without specifying its particular form or how it will come to us. We don't need to force it, just to let the energy flow. When the little fearful voice within us tries to tell us that this might not work, there is no need to give energy to that thought.

7. Making Money

Money is energy, and energy always returns to its origin. Human beings are goal-seeking creatures, constantly dealing with the need for growth and change. The wealthier we become, the more comfortable we can be, and the result can be the ability to be more creative and be of greater help to those around us. Of course, we can have all the money in the world and not be happy. It all depends on our relationship to our wealth.

I left my country, my family, and my native culture in search of wealth. I knew that when I became richer in mind, body, and spirit, I would be able to make more of a difference in the world as a whole. I would like to believe that I have succeeded in doing so. If I haven't, then the wealth I have achieved will have been of little significance.

8. Learning to Listen

There are three types of listening. The first one is hearing, but not really listening. Eighty percent of people practice this type. The second type of listening is when we are contentedly in conversation with others. This is listening in the common sense of the word. The third type of listening is intuitive. It's listening to our inner voice, a calm form of communication that goes beyond words.

When we use this intuitive faculty in listening, then we know what we know, and can make decisions more easily based on our gut feeling. This skill of using our intuition comes from the subconscious mind. I call it the heart of hearts. To get in touch with this faculty, all we have to do is to sit down and be quiet for a half an hour, doing absolutely nothing—no TV, no phone—just closing our eyes and listening to our breathing. This practice brings joy, calmness, relaxation, and laughter, and isn't that what all of us want?

Laura Day, in her book, *Practical Intuition*, writes:

Because, as adults, we have lost touch with our ability to fantasize and pretend, we have ironically cut ourselves off from our unconscious ability to provide us with meaning precisely when, with intellectually maturity, it is potentially most useful to us.

We don't recognize our intuition because it speaks to us in a different language. As a result, we dismiss it and ignore it. I can't estimate how many times I ignored my inner voice when I had to take action or make a critical decision in my professional or personal life. As a result, I missed out on many opportunities. Exercising our intuition will improve our decision-making and our thinking. Our rational mind will always try to interfere with our intuitive mind, but professionals such as doctors, lawyers, investment consultants, and even real estate agents like me routinely use this intuitive faculty for making diagnoses, exploring the entanglements of a case, assessing the merits of an investment, or reading customers' behavior. I have dealt with many businesspeople that use this faculty, and the results of my transactions with them have always been successful.

Not all of us have great instincts or intuition. Some of us are so busy working to help others grow that we forget about ourselves and our needs or desires. But if we are listening to that intuitive voice within us, it is important not to ignore it or close our ears to it, but to act upon it. Sometimes we can't make a decision based on facts alone. I often say, "Don't give me the facts; give me the truth." Messages coming from our heart will often be at complete variance with the facts or circumstances in our lives.

9. Valuing Ourselves

If we don't value ourselves, others will not value us. Love is putting the highest value on something, whether it is another person, a cause, our self, or life itself. Our love for one thing will affect our love for another. If we love ourselves, we will love others. If we don't love ourselves, we will attract people who will drag us down and sap our energy. When we lack energy, we will feel angry, fearful, and disconnected, and when people sense this about us, they will withdraw from us.

I lived through a period in my life when I had anxiety attacks. I couldn't breathe. I was hyperventilating. Customers didn't want to do business with me. I went to the doctor, and he gave me something to relax, but in reality it made me feel worse.

One day, I was watching television, and turned to a Christian network that has become a regular viewing channel for me. After listening to this broadcast, I felt calmer, renewed, re-energized, and reborn with the confidence to face people with enthusiasm, compassion, and understanding, and focus on their needs rather than my own.

It took a long time, but eventually people began to be attracted to me and want to do business with me once again. I forgave myself for the mistakes I had made, and also forgave those people who had offended or rejected me in the past. A new meaning of life arose within me. I let go of my bitterness, anger, and frustration, and this created a great emotional energy that started attracting people and money to me like a magnet.

10. Laughing, Smiling!

Anyone who knows me knows that I laugh a lot. When I was younger, I enjoyed stories and situations that made me laugh. Then I grew up and faced some of the hard knocks of adulthood, and for a while laughter took a backseat to tears and frustration. When I changed my attitude and outlook, the laughter returned, and now I laugh all the time. For me, laughter is healing, because it helps me to not take life or life's circumstances so seriously. This is not to say we should treat life frivolously or superficially. It simply means that when we find humor in our day-to-day life and can laugh, either at our mistakes or at circumstances around us, we will feel less stress and our burdens will seem lighter.

If we can't generate laughter, then a similar benefit can be gained from simply smiling...at work, on the bus, or in the grocery line. The nice thing about smiling, even at strangers, is that generally we get a smile back.

Hugs work, too, as Leo Buscaglia, the hug master proved. In cultures like my own, hugging and kissing are commonplace. It's difficult for me to understand people who don't spontaneously practice these outward signs of affection. It creates warmth between two people that, while it may last only a few seconds, is nevertheless healing. When we embrace life, face each day squarely, infuse it with passion, and find joy in the present, our success factor will grow accordingly.

11. Getting a Perspective on Our Problems

Whenever I have faced difficult situations, I have found that one way to minimize the stress is to consider the problems that other people are facing. Dr. Wayne Dyer offers a good technique along these lines. He suggests that we imagine that we are floating above the earth, but close enough to see all that is going on down below us. We see chaos, war, death, destruction, torture, poverty, hunger, and disease. Making these earthly observations helps us put our own problems into perspective. Our own problems suddenly won't seem so great in comparison to those of others.

Another way to accomplish this is to find a quiet place to meditate on our entire life, from the beginning to the present. In the entire scheme of our life, how big is the problem we now face? Have we ever faced anything bigger or more stressful before? How did we overcome that difficulty? When we see how we passed through previous problems, the current one may not seem so insurmountable.

12. Making Our Actions Authentic

We are rightly judged not by what we say but by what we do. We can promise just about anything, but delivering on that promise can be tricky sometimes. It's therefore important to have clarity and certainty in our mind before we act. Real thinking is gathering the right information about what we want to do. It's said that two percent of the people in the world know how to think, three percent think that they can think, and the other ninety-five percent die and go to heaven, and then they think! Real thinking, which is the highest paying job in the world, takes effort. Making our actions authentic requires this kind of real thinking.

13. Being Open to Others
The road to success can be a lonely one, but it doesn't have to be. If we have a mentor, counselor, life coach, or even a religious figure to turn to when questions or challenges arise, they can be very helpful. There are many such people in the world. We just have to have a mind that is willing, open, and receptive enough to learn from their experience. With a positive mental attitude and the company of people who share our beliefs, philosophy, and virtues in life, we will have the ingredients necessary to achieve our goals.

14. The Three P's
The three P's—persistence, patience, and perseverance—have worked for me throughout my life. I had an elderly friend who used to vacation in one of my rental properties. She always had flowers on her table and plants in the yard. One year, when she left, I noticed a yellow daisy plant on the porch ready to be tossed into the garbage. My favorite flowers are daisies and carnations, so I picked up the plant and decided to experiment with it. I wanted to give life back to this plant; it was wilted, and some of its stalks were dead, but I felt that it still had some life in it. I brought it home and replanted it, trimming off the dead leaves, watering it, and talking to it. I gave it my positive, nourishing thoughts, and I spent time watching it grow into a full-blown beautiful plant. It bloomed for another two years until Hurricane Wilma killed it.

That's what happens in our lives, too. When we nurture our soul, spirit, and mind, we give them life until the time comes when our Heavenly Father calls us home. If we take care of our self-image, nurture it with positive thoughts by planting good seeds in our mind, and mix it with a burning desire to achieve our goals, then all we have to do is to wait patiently, and one day all our nurturing will produce tangible results, and we will become successful. My philosophy is to never give up.

Some of my role models are the successful women in the Bible, such as the one described in Psalm 31: "She gets up while it is still dark; she provides food for her family..." The price of success can be steep. It can take years for our vision to take shape. We may often be impatient at our apparent lack of progress and our desire for greater results, but the time we invest in mastering what we like to do and doing it will pay off someday.

15. Prayer

Prayer and meditation are powerful tools, but they are not enough; we must act in order to get where we want to go, be what we want to be, know what we want to know, and have what we want to have. A Swedish proverb says, "God gives every bird a worm, but He does not throw it into the nest." The word "pray" is an action word. It means that if we pray for our life to improve, we must become a willing participant in achieving that goal. There is no point in praying for something unless we are willing to become part of the process of attainment.

I'm a firm believer in the premise that we can have our cake and eat it, too. Dreamers have a donut and concentrate on the hole. As guests on Earth, we have to put our hours and activities to good use, in order to be successful and productive.

16. The Three R's

There are pitfalls to success, and one of them is becoming overdeveloped in our career and professional life and underdeveloped in our personal life. If there is no balance between life and work, it's like trying to dance on one foot.

There comes a time when there's no fun or satisfaction in our success, and at that point we look in the mirror and ask what we can do to improve our situation. The answer is to allow time for the three R's—replenishing, restoring, and recuperating on a regular basis. When we give ourselves an hour or so daily for restful, nourishing moment, we are better able to reorganize, regroup, and reposition ourselves for productive effort and accomplishment.

14

Putting the REAL in Real Estate

I don't sell bricks and mortar.
I sell the essence of life here in the Florida Keys.

Lela Ashkarian

I WOULD BE totally remiss if I didn't devote a brief chapter to the real estate industry, which has given me such a rewarding career. My work as a realtor is fulfilling because I help people find their own piece of paradise. In the beginning, I didn't know what this country and this community had to offer me. I knew that I had a "can do" attitude. I worked into the wee hours of the morning studying maps, handpicking homes that were selling, and doing comparables for the right sales. In the long run, this country and its people have given me so much that I want to give back. I have received inspiration and pure love from friends, neighbors, managers, grocers, co-workers, attorneys, appraisers, and clients that is literally too great for words.

Early on, I learned that I had to do it myself, but that I also couldn't do it alone. I was selective with whom I entered into a business relationship. I made sure they had the same mindset and were in harmony with the system that I had developed to market and promote properties. I worked with people who were happy with the services that I rendered. I kept nurturing my strategic alliances, sharing with them, educating them, and being educated by them. I have a team of loan officers, inspectors, attorneys, and service providers on whom I depend to serve my clients just as I serve them. My customers are thrilled to refer others to me during and after the transaction.

Because English was my fourth language, I often had a problem keeping my thoughts together, but I was very patient and persistent in getting past this problem. My poor background was always my greatest motivating factor. My broker, Brian Schmitt, once asked me what kept me so enthusiastic, motivated, and charismatic. My response was, "I will never be poor again." When we treat our profession seriously and treat it as a business, we become a leader in our chosen field.

Real estate is a numbers game. I prospect five days a week *on* my business, and on the sixth day, I work *in* my business. Prospecting means calling on people whom I know or who have found me either through my website or through mutual friends, neighbors, acquaintances or business associates. I increase my referrals by staying in touch with my customers, truly connecting with them, and understanding their needs.

The Love Business

I love what I do, and I do what I love; that secret of success escapes probably ninety-five percent of Americans, who toil at a job or career they dislike or in conditions that don't foster their growth. To those people who hate what they do, or go about their work in a robotic way just fulfilling the basic requirements to get a paycheck, I would say, "If you don't like your vocation, get out of it immediately! Find something you love to do and become a master in that particular area or profession." Among the lessons that I have learned in my real estate business is that I'm truly in the "love business." When you love your job, it's easy. I love my profession, and am happy and grateful that I've succeeded in doing what I love to do.

When I get discouraged about not being able to get a listing or close a sale, I remember that I'm in the love business. The less I resist it, the quicker I will reach my goals. Release, relate, and relax; the good things will fall into place. All things come together for good when our intentions are good. We receive in proportion to what and how much we give. It's the law of cause and effect. We should never worry about what we're going to get, but rather concentrate on what we're going to give. When we plant seeds, we have to honor the gestation period. Just because we can't see anything above ground yet, doesn't mean that nothing is happening. As Hebrews 11:1 says, "Faith is the substance of things hoped for, the evidence of things not seen."

Goals

Whether it rains or shines, whether hurricanes come or go, I have one purpose and one goal, and that is to make a difference by serving the Higher Power. A goal is merely a slice of pie from our vision, and our vision is the pie of our life purpose. We all strive to achieve goals. It's natural for us to do so. Setting goals fires our inner self with enthusiasm, which furnishes us with energy. We all need both short-and long-range goals. Working on short-range goals gives us the confidence and patience that we need to work on the long-range goals until we achieve them.

A technique for programming the future involves writing down ten things we personally want to achieve. We can take each goal separately, and ask ourselves why it is important for us and what we will gain by achieving it. If we're merely trying to impress our boss or co-workers, it may not be a goal worthy of achieving. If it involves making the difference in the lives of other people, however, chances are that we will achieve that goal and much more.

In *The Science of Getting Rich*, Wallace D. Wattles explains the difference between having a competitive mind and having a creative mind. He recommends that we ask ourselves several questions in order to help us set proper goals. These include: What is the single most important thing I could create in my life right now? What is the best and highest use of my time at this moment? What qualities do I hope to gain by having these goals? When we ask ourselves these questions, our subconscious mind goes to work for us to achieve what we have set our sights on.

If our goals are not big enough to frighten us, then they are not true goals. They should loom ahead of us like huge mountains, high cliffs, or deep oceans, requiring determination to get to the other side. If we have nowhere to go, no challenging goal to achieve, what's the point in getting out of bed in the morning? It's also important, however, to be careful of what we ask for. If, for instance, we want to have someone to love, then we need to include "and who also loves me" in that wish. This rule is just as true when it comes to business. I have to fall in love with my clients to do business with them, and they in turn have to fall in love with me as their agent.

Akhurian Children's Hospital

Prospects

In the real estate business, an agent can't collect a commission until they make a sale. They can't write the offer until they have had a showing or made a presentation. And they can't have the showing or presentation until they have made the call. The foundation of the business, therefore, is in making the calls. For this, it is necessary to approach the customer with an open heart.

I don't try to sell my clients. I put myself in a relaxed state and make up my mind that if I give them what they want, they will respond in a positive way. I fall in love with my clients' wants, needs, and desires by putting positive energy into realizing their goals. When I practice this technique, my clients fall in love with me. They are drawn to me magnetically and refer other customers to me.

When I interview a buyer or a seller, I tell them how I work and what I will do for them to make their life easier. I gain an understanding of their needs and desires, what makes them unique, their special talents, and their passions. All of this energizes me to do my best for them. It's a team effort. I ask my clients to communicate to me their vision of their dream home, and then we develop the steps to achieve that goal. During my presentations, I make sure to convey to the homeowner that when I agree to show their property, I speak for them and represent their best interests. Property owners want an agent that will not misrepresent them. They look for such qualities as enthusiasm, tenacity, persistence, and honesty.

Non-Linear Thinking

I'm convinced that it's necessary to have a non-linear way of thinking in the real estate business. That means being unconventional and creative, sometimes taking radical steps, and always trying to look at things from a different angle. At times, I've gotten frustrated when things were not happening the way I expected, especially in marketing my services. I would be doing everything right—sending cards, prospecting on the phone, doing direct marketing, educating myself, and staying positive. Still, I wouldn't see any results. Nothing visible was occurring. Finally, I started understanding the laws of the universe and began to honor the gestation period for success.

For instance, let's say I was trying to get a listing by prospecting, advertising, and all the other techniques practiced by my associates in the business. This is the linear approach—doing the same thing and getting the same result. If none of these were working, I might go outside my comfort zone and begin a non-linear action, facilitating a FSBO (For Sale By Owner) by educating an individual on how to make a sale without listing their property with me, having faith that they, in turn, would refer me to their neighbors and family members.

I try to see myself right at the upper edge of success, like a kernel of popcorn in boiling oil, so hot that it's almost ready to pop. I don't judge myself when I'm in the middle of trying to make a sale. I don't evaluate myself by what I have not done by conventional means. The numbers don't represent *me*. Because I'm unconventional and thinking in a non-linear way about doing business, there is no way but to succeed.

The joy is in the process of the journey, not the destination. The goal is progress, not perfection. Linear thinking always dwells on money. Non-linear thinking emphasizes how I can serve the customer, how I can love what I am doing, how free I can feel, doing something different, being authentic, honoring myself, and honoring God. I don't just depend on God to take care of everything. Rather, I'm continually moving, making things happen.

Effective Marketing

Having a website that offers prospective clients and current customers access to vital information about listings and keeps them up to speed on doing business with me has worked for me like a stroke of genius. I keep it fresh and interesting, so that regular visitors to my site don't become bored. My mission statement is a succinct introduction to my way of doing business and what I expect from relationships with my business clients. With the global impact of the Internet, marketing through a website is highly effective. I've received great customers from all over the United States and the world at large just from people browsing my website. I can hardly imagine how long it would have taken me to find those people through more traditional forms of prospecting!

Mission Statement

My mission is to provide a smooth, understandable, and stress-free experience when helping someone buy or sell a home. I treat all of my clients the way I would like to be treated. I listen to each person with a true desire to understand his or her wants and needs, and I offer exceptional service and respect, which is what we all deserve and should expect from each other. I work every day to focus on my clients' goals. I fully explain all options available in every situation, giving them the knowledge they need to make informed decisions. In exchange for this high level of service, I expect my clients to refer me to their friends, family, and work associates.

A noted life coach, Stephen Covey, has written that we tend to trust people for two reasons: because they have character and because they are competent. Both are vital qualities. If they have one but lack the other, then we will tend not to trust them. My mission statement is a reflection of this principle, embodying both my character and competence. It means that my clients can trust me to provide them with the best possible service.

Success

My "hero" is Lela Ashkarian. I have molded myself into the person I am, in the same way that God created me in His image. As Stephen Covey said in one of his lectures, "I believe that when we were born, our work was born with us." Every couple of years, when I feel that I want to expand, that I no longer fit the position that I'm occupying, I do something different and exciting. I like to be around people who know more than I do, who have more experience than I have had, who have more money, a higher position in life, more intelligence, more patience, and so forth. To enjoy the same success as these people, I strive to be honest, audacious, detail-oriented, confident, authentic, happy, caring, persistent, understanding, and committed to continued growth. These virtues, I feel, will bring me to the top of the pyramid where there won't be any competition, merely the certainty, clarity, and freedom to enjoy the fruits of my labor. In a sense, all things are created twice, meaning we begin with an end in mind and are bonded with our goal again when it comes to pass.

My life coach, Bob Proctor, has said, "Don't slow down; calm down." This is how I measure my success: by progressive realization. If I have a worthy goal, a purpose in life, and focus on my personal goals and those of my clients, then I can take the time to count my blessings in the meantime.

I suggest to other agents to read at least two books a month that educate their mind and spirit. In his book, *The Greatest Salesman in the World*, Og Mandino says, "You have mastered the art of living not for yourself alone, but for others, and this concern has stamped thee above all as a man among men."

If there's one thing I dislike about the real estate business it's dealing with dishonest, disloyal people who think they can outsmart me. In such cases, I use my God-given intuition and boldness to look them in the eyes and tell them I can't work with them. I let such people go, because I prefer to spend my precious time assisting honest and loyal clients.

Another thing I dislike about the real estate business is that when things go wrong, the seller or buyer points their finger at the only person they know, and that's *me*! That's why I have prepared a list of reactions to avoid when a transaction goes sour, which I hand to clients before we enter into a working relationship.

15

Achieving Our Dreams

The future belongs to those
Who believe in their dreams.

Eleanor Roosevelt

I N MY YOUTH, when I was growing up, we had a scavenger
hunt game, and had great fun playing it. By way of analogy,
many of us are aware of our dreams and goals, but are
unconscious of the secret deadlines we have attached to them. We
spend our adult lives on what amounts to an extended scavenger
hunt, trying to gather our "must haves" according to a secret
timetable that reflects our values and lifestyle.

One night, when I was fourteen, I had a dream. In it, I knelt on
the hard concrete floor of our house and prayed to God: "Lord,
when I become a self-made millionaire, I will open a children's
hospital somewhere, I know not where." That dream came true in
October 2004. I was sitting in my office when Spirit spoke to me:
"This is the time. Act now." I started by searching the Armenian
Relief Society (ARS) on the Internet, and when I found their
website, I learned that the president of ARS happened to be from
my native community of Anjar, in Lebanon. They were just
breaking ground for the Akhurian Children's Hospital in Yerevan,
Armenia. I contacted them and began donating to that project.

On April 26, 2005, I attended the grand opening of the hospital,
accompanied by my sister-in-law and one of my nephews, Vartan
Tashjian, who played a big role in Armenia and its independence.

My childhood dream turned out to be no fantasy at all, but a commitment. Vartan is a reporter, writer, and public speaker. He wrote about our journey to Armenia, telling how he accompanied me the first time I stepped on the soil of the Biblical homeland of our ancestors, which a devastating earthquake in 1988 had left in ruins, killing more than twenty-thousand people and destroying towns and villages.

At the time, Armenia was at war with Azerbaijan, and Turkey had imposed a blockade against Armenia, so the government didn't have the resources to rebuild devastated areas. The situation remained critical even at the time I visited. The health center for mothers and babies that I sponsored is located in Akhurian, the poorest and most remote village in the Shirak region, the area destroyed by the earthquake. The people in that village live in prehistoric conditions, with no electricity or paved roads. Until this center was opened, there was no health care at all. The nearest hospital was an hour's drive away in an area where roads are usually blocked in winter due to heavy snow.

The center was a blessing to the villagers. The Armenian Relief Cross of the U.S.A. took the initiative in constructing it. I was particularly happy to see the joy of the villagers upon my arrival. During my visit, I went to see the major churches of Armenia and wept when I prayed in those sanctuaries so many centuries old.

I still live in the heart of the Florida Keys, where I first came to live with Richard Allen. Every morning, I start my day very early by reading the Bible. Then I step outside my seaside cottage to watch another beautiful sunrise. The gentle ocean breeze sweeps across my cheeks and seagulls fly overhead while I praise God for His goodness and mercy. I sing silent songs of gratitude for the magnificence of nature.

When I look back, I still remember the hard times but no longer feel the pain. I appreciate freedom having had the experience of once being bound. I am grateful that women in America can express themselves freely compared to those in my native culture. I made up my mind as a young woman that I would do whatever it took to move away from that society, and as it turned out I fulfilled my dream. We can accept where we have been planted or uproot ourselves and re-plant ourselves in a place that will enable us to grow to new heights. We can be "settlers," stuck in a rut, or we can become trailblazers. As Les Brown said, "Follow the trail, and when there is no trail, make one."

Sometimes, we find ourselves caught between desire and obedience, between our dreams and our sense of duty. When we ignore the message that comes from within our heart to do what we desire, to follow our dream, the price is always too high. Did I pay dearly for my bad choices? Yes, indeed. My young husband, Vatche, was cute, smart, articulate, multi-talented, and generous, but I overlooked the fact that he put his desires, wishes, and dreams ahead of any that we had in common.

When it comes to relationships, it pays to carefully study the other person's motivations. This doesn't mean becoming judgmental, but merely being realistic, understanding the role our potential partner plays in our life, and comprehending the intent of our relationship with them. The deeper we dig, the more we understand and evaluate their character, then the easier it will be to find a route to a healthy relationship. It helps to ask why we attract people with certain behavior or qualities. Asking the right question will lead to the right answer. It's better to have a short, bad relationship than a long one.

I didn't have the same dreams, goals, or purpose as Richard or Vatche. Richard wanted to sail the world; I wanted to be grounded on dry land. Vatche also had his own agenda for his life that didn't match mine. If we meet someone we feel is the right person, it's wise to make it our intention to be in alignment with that person's dreams and goals. If we don't do that, we will find ourselves looking through the same window as our partner, but viewing a completely different scene.

Being in alignment with the right life partner doubles any blessing that we may have in our lives. As David Viscott once wrote, "To love and be loved is to feel the sun from both sides." However, such alignment doesn't come about without effort on our part. We can't expect people to do what we aren't doing for ourselves, to be generous when we are stingy, to be gracious when we are unkind, to be affectionate when we are cold, to show respect when we are domineering, or to applaud us when we are critical of them.

I have lived my life without regrets. Everything that has happened to me has made me the woman I am today. Scars have surrendered to smiles, and loss has been redeemed by love. True to my Armenian roots, I am passionate about life, and I look forward to where my passion will take me next.

To contact Lela, visit her website: www.MyHomesInTheKeys.com

Tempest-tossed souls,
Wherever ye may be,
Under whatsoever conditions
Ye may live,
Know this –
In the ocean of life,
The isles of blessedness
Are smiling,
And the sunny shore
Of your ideal
Awaits your coming.
Keep your hand
Firmly upon the helm
Of thought.
In the back of your soul
Reclines the commanding Master:
He does but sleep;
Wake Him.
Self-control is strength.
Right thought is mastery;
Calmness is power.
Say unto your heart,
"Peace, be still."

James Allen
As a Man Thinketh

Made in the USA
Columbia, SC
05 June 2020